WHEN NEWARK
HAD A
CHINATOWN

My Personal Journey

by

Yoland Skeete-Laessig

Edited by Hal Laessig

DORRANCE
PUBLISHING CO
EST. 1920
PITTSBURGH, PENNSYLVANIA 15238

The contents of this work, including, but not limited to, the accuracy of events, people, and places depicted; opinions expressed; permission to use previously published materials included; and any advice given or actions advocated are solely the responsibility of the author, who assumes all liability for said work and indemnifies the publisher against any claims stemming from publication of the work.

Dorrance Publishing Co
585 Alpha Drive
Suite 103
Pittsburgh, PA 15238
Visit our website at www.dorrancebookstore.com

ISBN: 978-1-4809-1036-2
eISBN: 978-1-4809-1358-5

1- My Grandfather Lionel Sheafe (Chan), in his World War 1 uniform, 1914. This book is dedicated to his memory. Courtesy the author.

2- My Uncle Ming as a very young man. Circa early 1900's. My grandfather and he were inseparable. Courtesy the author.

CONTENTS

PREFACE

First of all, let me say that I am not a historian, nor am I a scholar, nor have I ever claimed to be one. The writings I have presented here are based on events that occurred from 1994 to the present and are my experiences, feelings and conclusions from my research to find a history of Newark Chinatown. The story is punctuated with an examination of my own Chinese ancestry and my experiences as a child growing up on an island where, as a Chinese member of the Parliament said, "If you count all the people of Chinese ancestry and mixed Chinese ancestry in Trinidad as Chinese, you will have the largest segment of the population of the Island." This book is about my fascination with Chinese culture stemming from my being raised by my Chinese grandfather and other relatives with whom I spent the early part of my life and who played a very important role in how I learned to view the world. My grandfather was a very loving man who would hide me in his carpenter shop to play or take me to the horse stables with him instead of taking me to school. During the first five years of my life I spent every day with him so that when he died—I was five—my whole world collapsed. My personality changed and I experienced deep emotional pain for the first time.

Because of the prevalent role race has become in our social global community, I have had to spend my years without an identity. I am African, Asian, and European. As the world becomes more multiethnic, the psychological problems I faced growing up and the economic barriers this presented are disappearing. I hope they will fade away forever so that future generations will not have to see color and race before they see the person. It is for this reason I was driven to pursue this quest. I was amazed that a race of people could have disappeared so completely from an area in which there once had lived 3,000. I was amazed that no one cared about this. I was amazed that no historical marker or plaque stood on the spot where they had walked. But then that is the way of the history of all humanity. People come and people go. So when you read this, think of it as a story someone is telling you as they sit across from you, perhaps in a coffee shop or café, because it is my journey through a part of Newark's history.

I would like to thank Eduardo Almeida, for introducing me to Betty Lee Sung and for his extensive research into the deeds of the very many properties owned by Chinese in the heyday of Newark Chinatown; I would like to thank Betty Lee Sung for my first starting lessons in researching this history; Norma Eng Wong for teaching me to make sticky rice and for being "Norma"; Wally and Frank Soo Hoo for helping me to keep up my strength when things got down; Frank Eng for his constant supply of information; Ron Eng Young for copying all my materials; Robert Lee for his frank insights into human behavior and friendship; The Kee Chee family; Jack Tchen, Director of the Asian, Pacific, American Institute, who acted as my mentor; Helen Zia, author, historian and a member of Newark Chinatown community; and to Leslie Eng, Dylan Yeats, and Sally Yerkovich, who helped start the first Newark Chinatown Reunion; and all the people of Newark Chinatown who came back to Newark yearly to celebrate *The Dragon Returns To Newark*, five years in a row.

A special thanks to John Richards and Baraka Sele of NJPAC for their Mellon Grant to start the project; to Ye Xun for his incredible work in creating the models of Newark Chinatown; to Richard Eng of the Eng Association for believing in me; to Corky Lee for his photographic documentation and support; and most importantly my husband Hal Laessig, without whom I could not have done any of this.

Thanks also to: Newark Public Library, NJ Room and especially Robert Blackwell who worked there at the time, the Newark Historical Society, the New Jersey Council on the Humanities, the Mid Atlantic Arts Foundation, the Asian Pacific American Institute, and the Tamiment Library, NYU, for archiving all the materials from my research.

3-Lun On Co Building, 204 Mulberry Street, 1990's, courtesy the author.

LOOKING FOR CHINATOWN - 1

Ming Chow

It was the usual quiet Sunday morning in 1994. Funny how dog walking is such a peaceful experience. While the dog sniffs at the ground, my eyes sniff at things above the ground and in the sky. I was becoming familiar with every nook and cranny, every curve, every arch, every name at the top of every building, on every stretch of my walk, on every day. Examining the turn of the century buildings was the most exciting aspect of the walk. The air was cool; it was late fall, and instead of the pinks of early sunrise the morning was a cool blue the kind of cool blue that makes all the colors and details of the buildings and the surroundings come to life. I had walked down this street so many times and each time I would discover something different.

I remembered this neighborhood when I first moved to Newark in 1979. Young's grocery store was still on Mulberry Street near the corner of Green Street. Even though I never went inside the store, I had sometimes seen Mr. Young and his elderly Chinese father who lived downstairs below the shop. Somewhere in my mind a childhood memory sparked of my own Chinese grandfather and my Uncle Ming. Directly cat-a-corner from Young's was Wah Hing Chinese restaurant, but these small shops never added up to anything in my mind.

The street had a solemnity from memories of a time when it was bustling with business and people. A time when the trolley tracks ran down the middle of the street, and on each side were mansions, once the town houses of Newark's business tycoons.

The grand, four-story brownstone, on the corner of Green and Columbia, now a rooming house, was the town house of a hat manufacturer. The small three-story house, right next to the restaurant on Green Street, still had the original stove and cooking fireplaces from when the house was built in the 1700s. This side of the city, close to City Hall, was separated from what was known as "Down Neck" by McCarter Highway and a railroad track that brought trains into and out of Newark Penn Station. The railroad track, built as part of the Great Pennsylvania Railroad during the beginning of the RR era in 1846, made a circle around the then German, Irish, and Italian immigrant neighborhood. Thus the area became known as the Ironbound. In 1979, I lived in an artists' loft on Green Street, on the Down Neck side of the tracks, in what had become the Portuguese section. At that time, anything on the opposite side of the tracks, the area where City Hall lay, was not my territory; I had been warned it was dangerous, so I would hurry on my way to Broad Street or any other place, moving carefully, keeping a watchful eye. But that was eleven years ago.

Now I lived in this neighborhood around City Hall and it was safe, not only because it was now my neighborhood, but because I had gotten to know the people here, had organized a community center, an arts and cultural space run by my husband and I. Together with the community we had made an effort to remove the drugs, the prostitution and make the neighborhood safe for families and elderly "roomers" renting rooms in the old nineteenth century homes. In 1991, I moved my artist studio into an old jewelry factory on the corner of Lafayette and Liberty Street. The building still had all the trimmings, inside and out, from the days when it held a collective of artisans, each making a particular part of a piece of jewelry. The aura of that time haunted the place, which was why I loved my loft.

In 1995, under very strange circumstances, I acquired a Chinese Chow dog. The Chow was the favorite dog of the bygone Chinese emperors. It was the guard dog and it was the hunting dog. It symbolized power, strength, extreme loyalty, and intelligence. All these were qualities in the personality of the Chow. At the time, I was teaching video and filmmaking at Brooklyn Technical High School. I usually left the loft around six o'clock each morning. One morning I stepped outside my front door and lying on the aged granite slab steps was a large, long-haired, golden- colored dog. He had the face of a bear. I had never seen one of his kind. He was directly in my path but out of the way of the opening door. He made no effort to move for me to pass, so I had to step around and over him, which I did, so as not to disturb him. After I stepped over him I bent down to take a look at him. He ignored my attempt at eye contact and looked away into the distance. He seemed tired.

"Hey," I said to the dog, "what are you doing here?"

No answer, no movement.

"Boy, you look tired and hungry. Where did you come from?"

The dog continued to avoid me.

I walked around him again, went back into the house and brought out some food, a left-over portion of stew from the night before, in my favorite Japanese bowl. I put the bowl in front of him and immediately, without moving a muscle of his huge frame, he put his mouth into the bowl and hungrily lapped up the food. I picked up the bowl and, stepping over him, took it back into my kitchen and returned to the front steps. He was still lying there unmoved. I did not try to touch him; he did not want to be touched. He seemed sad and lost and yet indifferent to any desire for pity, so I said goodbye and went to work. I completely forgot about the dog once I left and did not think about him all day. As I returned that evening, Mario, the Italian carpenter whose shop was directly across the hallway, looked out from his door slightly ajar and said, "A dog came into the building and slept at your door all day." I was surprised. I laughed, but paid it no mind and went about my business.

Hours later I went to Seabra's grocery store several blocks away to get something I needed. Returning, I crossed McCarter Highway and walked up the grade to Liberty Street. I saw the long golden-haired animal coming down Lafayette Street toward me. His face was the face of a golden bear curving around a black spot which was his nose, his head held high and proud. I was immediately struck by the grace and flow of his body as he softly padded in my direction. Liberty Street stood between us, and at this moment Teresa Silva came driving down the street in her ruby-colored Lincoln. Teresa Silva was from Galicia in Spain. She was outspoken, took care of the neighborhood, and lived in a three-story, red brick townhouse built in the late 1800's that had never been changed. Her parents had immigrated to this neighborhood when she was a young girl. She had married and still lived in the same house, of which she was very proud. She was one of my neighbors who lived around the corner on Columbia Street. She stopped the car at the crosswalk, her round face and red-brown hair glistening in the sun as she stuck her head out of the window to watch the dog. The golden body moved silently, gracefully, crossing the walk in front of the car toward me.

Teresa yelled. "Grab him, grab him—grab that dog!"

Surprised at her statement, I looked at the dog, who by this time had come almost to my side. He walked up to my knee and I put my hand on his head and held his mane. It was thick and long, and, although dirty, it was soft.

"Grab him!" she called. "Everybody has been trying to catch that dog for days. He has no home, he's a stray," Teresa shouted. I held the dog's mane gently in my hand and led him to her car. He allowed me to do this.

"What are you yelling about Teresa?" I said to her.

We stood at her car, both of us, as she said looking down at him, "He is so beautiful. Keep him; he needs a home."

I looked down at the animal. Her words, "He needs a home," resounded in my head and I said internally, *Not me. I don't know this dog from Adam.*

"Everyone has been trying to catch this dog; he's been running around here for days," she repeated.

Funny I hadn't noticed him, I thought.

She continued, "He needs a home. Why don't you keep him?"

I said nothing as I listened to her ramble on about this. "Well, maybe we can find his owner," I said.

She laughed. "He is so beautiful." The dog opened his mouth and yawned; a purple-black tongue stretched out and pulled back in.

"See," said Teresa, "he has a purple tongue; he's a thoroughbred."

I hadn't the faintest idea what she was talking about, but the dog ended up being brought into my loft. My husband, on seeing the dog, said to me, "I don't want a dog."

"I don't either," I said, "but he can't stay on the street. He will get killed or taken for experimentation." At that time, there were lots of stray dogs appearing in the neighborhood that were picked up and used for experimentation.

"Let's try to find out who lost him. He has a collar," I said, reaching into his neck. I unbuckled what turned out to be a flea collar. It had a phone number on it. I immediately called the phone number, but by now it was late in the day and there was no answer.

Well, anyway, as the story goes, we searched everywhere, went on the internet, made calls to the pound and all the dog agencies looking for someone who had lost their Chinese Chow, and found nothing. By this time, he had been groomed by the local groomer who told us about his heritage and stated that he was obviously a dog who had been cared for because he was trained and his nails were clipped.

The days went by and turned into weeks and months and he stayed. My husband at first refused to care for him except to pet him for about a half hour every day when he came in the door after work. He still does so now, but he will occasionally walk and feed him when I travel.

I named the dog after my Chinese uncle, Ming, because I felt that he had been sent to guard me from danger. From the beginning, I felt something strange between this dog and myself. Something about him being on my doorstep, something about him being a Chinese Chow, the emperor's guard dog, the emperor's hunting dog. Chows are very independent dogs, and they are very particular about who they allow to touch or relate to them. We never had any problem with Ming, but during the early years with us he would not allow anyone except us to touch him. Ming eventually became more polite and learned to be more social, but was always his own person, and his aura demanded respect.

So here I was walking this dog on Lafayette Street on this overcast day. I turned to go down Mulberry towards Green Street, walking on the Broad Street side, past what used to be Perrett's watch store. As usual I moved slowly. As the dog grazed around the trees on the sidewalk and on the cement, my eyes grazed the surrounding buildings, taking in every cut, design, line in the brick. It was while doing this that I looked up and noticed something carved in the very top stone of one of the buildings. I stopped and tried to make out the letters and read the words "Lun

On Co." I stood looking in amazement. I read and reread the words sounding them out loud. The realization that this was a Chinese name moved slowly into my thoughts. I looked carefully at the building, the design elements, and then walked around it to look more carefully. It reminded me of the buildings I had seen in Cuba. The closed up areas of the windows on the second floor could not hide the fact that these had been doors that opened onto the elaborate fire escape. Many San Francisco buildings also had this design. But I had never seen this particular use of doors in any buildings on the East Coast. Why was a Chinese name carved in the stone at the top of a building in the middle of nowhere in Newark?

I walked back to the front of the building and looked at it to be sure I was not mistaken. Yes, it was "Lùn On Co." I began to speculate, looking at the rest of the neighborhood. Could this have been owned by a Chinese person? No other building bore any marks of Asian culture or design. There was the Chinese take-out restaurant around the corner on Green Street, but that looked like a "Johnny-come-lately" Chinese takeout with horrible food. With Ming now leading me home, I knew I had to find an answer.

Robert Lee, Director of the Asian American Art Center, attended our annual New Year's party that December. We had been friends for a few years, over which time we had become like family. I was talking to Bob and telling him about the name I saw at the top of the building. He looked at me in surprise and said, "This area used to be Newark's Chinatown; I was born here." I looked at him in amazement. When I could finally speak I started questioning him about the history as far as he knew. Bob was born and grew up on Court Street, just a few blocks from City Hall. The area had been destroyed and rebuilt to house the *Star Ledger Newspaper.* Bob was then a 5-foot-5, stocky "Chinaman" (spoken lovingly) with a thick black head of hair that hung around the sides of his head. He had graduated from Rutgers and moved into New York City where he had become involved with the 60's radical groups of the time, fighting for "Asian Power." It was in NYC he met his wife, Eleanor S. Yung, who did contemporary and classical Chinese dance. They were involved along with many others, in starting a group called Basement Workshop, which was the seminal Asian American arts and performance umbrella organization of the time. I had met Bob through Willie

6

Cole, the well-known Newark artist, when Willie was exhibiting at the Asian American Arts Center. Bob and I became fast friends after that. Now here we were at our annual New Year's party and I was learning things I had never known about Bob and the neighborhood. We tried to continue a discussion about the topic, but the noise made it difficult to talk, so I made an appointment to get together with him in the coming weeks. This was the start of my quest to find Newark's Chinatown.

It took several years of making phone calls, writing letters, attending many events, making contacts, and writing more letters. There is nothing I did not do to find out what I wanted to know about Chinatown, and now, years later, I still find that there is much more I still have to learn. Since I had never written a book before, I consulted many friends, particularly John Kuo Wei Tchen, Director of the Asian/Pacific American Studies at NYU, who became my mentor. At last, after many rewrites, here is a memoir of my experiences in my search for Newark Chinatown.

Looking for Chinatown

I have often asked myself, "How does one begin to look for something that doesn't exist; something that seems to have vanished into thin air?" The name at the top of the building was like a footprint in the sand and time was like the approaching wave getting ever closer to melt its existence. I became obsessed with the idea that somewhere this history must have been documented; somewhere I would find the story of this vanished group of people. First, I went where anyone would go to find information—the Newark Public Library, New Jersey Room. I asked for information on the Chinese who had lived in Newark. The librarian pulled out a file. The file had several clippings. I examined these, reading and devouring every word of what seemed to be negative, bigoted statements of murders, drug dealing, gambling, and illegal alien arrests. In between the lines I began to see stories of apartment houses at 10:30 at night, whose doors were axed in search of victims; a married couple dragged out of their wedding ceremony and jailed, having to send for their papers to show that they were legally American citizens. The more I read, the more dismayed I became.

I asked Charles Cummings why there weren't any good news stories. He pulled out a file showing me three clippings.

One was of the birth of a boy child named Paul to Norma Eng Wong in Chinatown, one was of a young woman, Mary Fong, sitting, pin up style, on a beautifully carved Chinese Chest, another, a story of a Chinese New Year celebration. That was the extent of the good news. One day I took my video camera and had a long interview with Bob Lee, in which he told me about growing up in Newark and who was still living there.

I continued my search, happy that there were still a few Chinese living in the neighborhood. Jack Mon lived right next door to me; how could I have missed that? I had seen him and several elderly Chinese men leaving and entering his house but had never said any more than good morning or good evening. With the help of Bob Lee, I made a list of all the Chinese who lived in the area. Frank Eng was one, and Yang Shing was another. Bob said I should definitely talk to Frank, so I introduced myself and became fast friends with Frank, who was a wealth of information. Frank invited me to dinner for Chinese New Year and introduced me to several men who had grown up in Newark Chinatown. The story had finally begun.

I began to collect names of people and stories, oral histories, and old photographs. I had to fill in the gaps however, since these men belonged to a generation that grew up in Newark just prior to or after World War II and had no real knowledge of the history of the first immigrants. It was important to find why the Chinese had come to Newark. What had brought them here? I knew about the Chinese building the railroads, but why and how Chinese got to other parts of the United States was unknown to me. I discovered that most of the Chinese who settled in Newark were Engs. Frank was an Eng and he knew quite a bit of his own family history and that was a big help. Talking to Frank and scouring the library history books helped me to piece the historical immigration story together. Frank introduced me to the elders from the old community. As I spoke to the elders I began to get a story of the history of China and the economic conditions in the villages from which their fathers and grandfathers—and my great-grandfather—came. I began to hear the stories of the men and women who left their towns and homes in the old country and struggled to survive and flourish in a time and place that had somehow emerged, thrived, and then vanished.

PART 1

LIFE IN CHINA

伍子胥太祖真像

4- *Early Eng Clan Leader, from The Eng Association Yearly Publication, courtesy Richard Eng, Eng Assoc.*

像遺君太劉配德公雲章伍

嶺南伍氏總譜　卷十

5- *Early matriach of Eng Clan, from The Eng Clan Association Yearly Publication, courtesy Richard Eng, Eng Assoc.*

I

A BRIEF LOOK AT CHINESE HISTORY 1644 TO 1864

Around 1644, the Ming Dynasty ended and the Manchus took over North China, establishing the last imperial dynasty, the Qing. The Manchus realized that they had to accept and appropriate Ming/Han Chinese culture in order to control it, so they retained many of the Chinese and Confucian practices, laws, and rituals and reappointed many Ming officials to their former positions. However, their fear of total assimilation and their desire for total control made them adopt laws against intermarriage between Manchus and the predominant Han Chinese. Manchus were forbidden to do manual labor or be involved in merchant trade or in local government positions. In 1644, when the Manchus took Beijing, the Ming resistance tried in vain to restore the Ming dynastic rule. Insurrections followed, led by the scholars, philosophers, and officials who were Ming supporters. In May of 1645, in their march to regain control of all of China, the Qing are said to have killed over 800,000 people in a ten-day massacre. Further resistance continued, spurred on by a decree issued in 1644 in which all Chinese males were ordered to shave the front of their heads and wear a queue, a single long braid, as a sign of servitude to the new Qing Emperor. As attempts to reestablish a Ming dynasty failed, remaining Ming forces retreated to Taiwan, making raids on southern coastal cities to replenish supplies. From 1661 to 1669, in the province of Guangdong, ethnic Punti villagers were forced by the Manchus to move inland to deny any resources to the remaining Ming forces. Those who refused to move were killed, and houses, towns, and cities were burned to the ground. The purge brought with it such devastation that although Chinese were forbidden to immigrate many had already begun to do so.

With the coastal areas depopulated, the Manchus began a program of relocating ethnic Hakka populations from other parts of China to re-settle the area. In the coming centuries, this program would have disastrous results.

Beginning in the sixteenth century, under the Ming Dynasty, southern China had developed extensive trade with the rest of the world, with Western merchants navigating from the Straits of Malacca, establishing their trading posts at Macau and the southern costs of Guangdong. With the forced relocation in Guangdong, many local Chinese retreated to Taiwan, but the first Chinese to reach North America may have been those who traveled on Spanish galleons to the Philippines and Spanish colonies of the West Coast of America. As time went on, European traders, soon to be followed by missionaries, increasingly came, bringing Western values and learning to Chinese culture and, in return, bringing an appreciation for Chinese culture and luxury goods back to the West. With the increase in maritime trade, the first Cantonese immigrants found their way on merchant ships to the Caribbean and the East Coast of America in the 1700s.

As European desire for Chinese "things and goods" —tea, porcelain, and silk— increased, the desire to trade with China increased. The Chinese Emperor, however, felt China needed nothing that the rest of the world had. By the early 1800s, the British had become addicted to all things Chinese. The Qing administration, however, allowed no imported goods and demanded that payment for Chinese goods be only in silver bars. By this time, the British maritime merchants had already been importing opium from India into China through the black market. To offset the imbalance of trade, the British decided to increase the import of opium. In small quantities at first, and along with Indian cotton, the British illegally traded opium in Chinese ports, despite the fact that this business was strictly prohibited by Chinese law. In order to understand the nightmare that was befalling China at this time, one has to examine carefully how these sales could be transacted.

By previous treaty regulations, China allowed British civil servants into specific posts in the government. These agents, working with corrupt Chinese merchants and officials, secured the passage of increasingly large amounts of opium into the population, creating total havoc and disaster for the Chinese people. Guangdong was the center of this trade and the resulting social upheaval. In 1839, as a result of the confiscation of 20,000 chests of opium and the detention of the entire foreign community by a Chinese official named Commissioner Lin Zexu, the British retaliated with an offensive in Guangdong that started the First Opium War. The victories of the British in the two Opium Wars began the downfall of the Chinese empire and the creation of China as a colony of the British Empire focused on Guangdong.

The weakening of Qing prestige and authority following the defeat by the British led in turn to increased corruption and social unrest. In Guangdong, and especially in the district of Toishan, the legacy of the Hakka repopulation of the Punti coastal areas from two hundred years before resulted in social conflict as these populations increased. In 1851, the Hakka-led Taiping Rebellion erupted in Guangxi province to the south, and soon there was rebellion and unrest in all of southern China. On opposing sides, clan warfare erupted between the Cantonese Punti and Hakka, lasting over ten years and resulting in the deaths of over a million people through war and famine and the destruction of thousands of villages. (Lambert M. Surhone, Mariam T. Tennoe, and Susan F. Henssonow, *Punti-Hakka Clan Wars*: Gardners Books. 2011).

During the massive conflict, captives were sold to the Spanish and transported to Cuba and South America. Refugees began to find passage to California to escape the conflict and to send money back to the devastated villages they left behind.

6-A house in Toisan, circa 1990's, courtesy Daisy Soo Hoo.

7-A kitchen inside a Toisanese home, circa 1990's, courtesy Daisy Soo Hoo.

*8-Entrance Door to home in the village of Toisan, circa 1990's courtesy Daisy Soo
Hoo.*

9-The Village of Toisan, circa 1990's courtesy Daisy Soo Hoo.

II

How the Chinese Left Guandong

Of the immigrants who came to the Americas from China during the eighteenth and nineteenth centuries, most came from the area of Toishan, in the district of Sunning, in the province of Guangdong, northeast of the port city of Canton. This entire area was experiencing drastic economic failure. In Toishan, village life was extremely difficult. Cantonese, mostly involved in fishing and trading, were sea travelers and among the few Chinese who traveled frequently to other ports and countries of the world. Word of gold found in California reached the ears of the villagers and traveling to acquire some of this gold seemed better than continuing in the poverty that the village offered. Hundreds of thousands of Cantonese contracted themselves out and boarded ships bound for anywhere they were told there was work and food to be had.

My own great-grandfather, an orphan boy of ten years, was sold to a French missionary family working in Canton. The missionaries finished their work in Canton and sailed for a French Caribbean Island to continue their work sometime between 1852 and 1860. Somehow, they stopped over in Trinidad and never left. My great grandfather lived with the missionary family, whose name was Begette, for many years, changed his name from Chan to Begette, and after years of work on their estate, left to make his own fortune. With the help of one of the Chinese associations in Trinidad, he bought a small shop and sent away to China for a wife.

The population of Canton, China, must have been larger than can be imagined since a continual flow of immigrants from this area populated the cities of the United States, the Caribbean, and many other places. As a result, the majority of recorded Chinese immigrants who entered the United States, Canada, and the Caribbean during this era came from this part of China.

19

During my research I discovered that a large number of Newark Chinatown residents carried the name Eng. Even those who had paper names of Lee, Young, and Wong were part of the Eng family or clan. This was one of the most prevalent of clans in Newark, Chinatown. Like many Chinese who came to America, they had bought false identities—paper names—in order to get traveling papers. Norma Eng Wong, the owner of the former Shanghai Restaurant in Newark Chinatown, often said about the Engs in Newark Chinatown, "If you dropped a brick out of the window, you would hit an Eng."

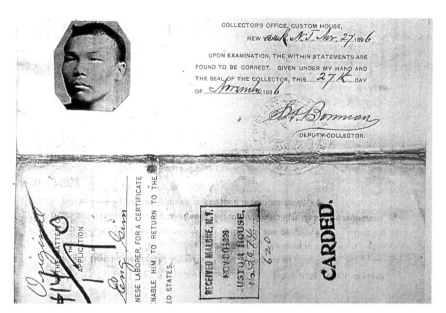

10- *Return Certificate for Frank Eng's Uncle dated 1896, courtesy National Archives.*

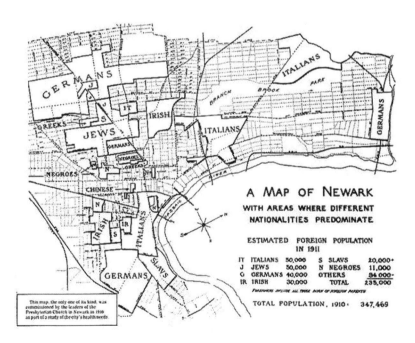

11-*Newark Map showing Chinese area, 1911, commissioned by First Presbyterian Church, Newark, NJ, courtesy Newark Public Library.*

III

FRANK ENG'S FAMILY

Frank was born at 202 Mulberry Street. He attended Lafayette Street School and East Side High. As a young boy, he worked in the Palais Joy, one of the major Chinese restaurants of the day located on Broad Street. He graduated from Cornell in 1958 and went on to get an MBA from Rutgers University, attended the University of Idaho where he received his MS, and continued his education, attending the University of Washington and MIT for post-doctoral studies. Now that he is retired, he has completed his Masters in Art History at New York University.

Chinese came to America as early as the sixteenth century in trading ships. Frank Eng has told me the story of how members of his family left Canton and traveled to California in one of these sailing ships. His family was in California around 1840 working for the descendants of Spanish Grandees. These were the upper class Spanish noblemen who had been given land grants in the seventeenth century by the Spanish government to settle what is now California and Mexico. These descendants of wealthy Spanish nobles had recruited Chinese laborers to work on their estates. During the time of the Gold Rush, Frank's great-great-grandfather left the farm to become a merchant to the panhandlers, who needed supplies as well as clothing. At this time the U.S. had no immigration laws. Chinese had been going back and forth to China from the U.S. for decades, bringing their children and their wives. Sometimes entire families, brothers, cousins, and their children traveled this route to find work.

Frank related to me that, in his research, he came across a Stanford University history of the Northern California Chinese in which he found a picture and story of the brother of his great-great-grandfather, who owned a grocery store in Monterrey, California. This was an exciting moment for Frank, especially since the book had photos of the Chinese merchant. As the railroads moved east, many Chinese continued working with the railroad companies, either laying tracks or maintaining the tracks and equipment to keep the railroads running. The Chinese were the only experienced work force that the railroad builders could depend on since many of them remained with these companies for several years as the railroads moved throughout the nation.

Frank states that Chinatowns were established in Baltimore (1780) and New York (1790) by Chinese who first went to the Caribbean and then came to the U.S. to continue their search for work. Frank's great-grandfather was named Eng Gim. He came to Newark as part of the group assigned to work in the Belleville laundry; however, he left the laundry and moved into the city of Newark and opened a business. He owned a grocery store on the corner of Green and Columbia Streets. This site is now a parking lot for Seabra grocery store trucks. He was a very successful merchant and because of this was able to travel back and forth to China, declaring his cash as $2,000 in 1896.

After the Chinese Exclusion Laws, Chinese men had to prove they were merchants with large savings in order to leave the country and return. The information provided here is a photo of Eng Gim from his papers allowing him to leave the country and return. The particular trip of which this paper is concerned is the trip in which Eng Gim was returning to China to bring back his son, Frank's grandfather. At this time, Chinese born in the U.S. did not have citizenship rights. Chinese who had children born in the U.S. often sent their children back to China to be educated. This is also true of Chinese men who had non-Chinese wives. Frank's grandfather had four sons and two daughters. Although Frank's father was born in San Francisco, he also was sent back to China to be educated. Frank states that his grandfather had married in San Francisco and worked in the Monterrey store before becoming part of the group that ended up in the Belleville laundry. After he left the laundry, he took up residence on Mulberry Street in Newark Chinatown, maintaining businesses in New York City as well. Frank is a tireless human being whose quest for knowledge will never end. I would often make an appointment to ask Frank questions about anything at all, but especially Chinese history, with my note pad, tape recorder and lots of time. My appointment would be over, my mind oversaturated, and questions still filling my head.

IV

THE ENG CLAN

The earliest written documents of the Eng or Wu clan date back to 1169. These Engs were descended from the Wu clan, whose seat was in Lujiang, Anhui. The Anhui Province is northeast of the Guangdong Province. When I discussed the Eng Diaspora with Frank Eng, he told me that the Eng family poem was the genealogy of all the Engs, and through this poem, each Eng could trace their ancestry back to the beginning. He also told me about Wolfram Eberhard's book *Social Mobility in Traditional China,* which proved to be the entire history of the Wu clan. At the Eng Association in New York City, I also found a book with photographs of the early Engs and the poem of which Frank spoke.

According to Eberhard, the Wu clan lived in the Anhui province until the fortieth and forty-third generations. They moved to Kaifeng in the Henan province during generations forty-three to fifty. From there they multiplied into four main houses that were known as the Ch'iu-kuan house, the P'u-t'ien branch, the Han-yuan house and the Lu-wei house. The Newark Engs are descended from the Lu-wei house.

The Lu-wei house lived in Hsin-ning (Guangdong Province) near Canton from the forty-ninth generation, which was before 1154. This house then produced the Jung-kui branch, which lived in Hsin-ning until generation fifty-three. Four of the members of generation fifty-one through fifty-six settled in Taishan and grew into a larger group until generation seventy-three. It was around this time that the migrations abroad began.

As Wolfram Eberhard stated in *Social Mobility in Traditional China:*

> The very large and greatly subdivided Lu-wei house started out
> as a landowning gentry family, always in civil or educational po-

sitions. They created more and more new settlements which they manned with such members of the family as were not interested in or capable of study. Because being in business was looked down on in Chinese culture, the first move into business did not begin until the 16th century, when trade became recognized as a valuable skill. In the 18th century the main house declined, and by the 19th century few men in this house were still in important jobs in the bureaucracy. At the same time, during this period, more and more of them were going into business. A certain inclination is to be seen toward drug stores and medicine in general; the trend toward geomancy disappears in the late 19th century. In the early 19th century, with the new possibilities given by the foreign powers, more and more men of the poorer settlements emigrated to South-East Asia, the Philippines and North and South America. Most of these returned to establish their own shops in South China. Towards the end of the 19th century, the descendants of these men entered the colleges in China or in the United States. In the 20th century more and more members of the house became teachers or at least helped in establishing schools; they shunned government jobs, although some were closely allied with Sun Yat-Sen and the revolutionaries. Many were local leaders in the 1930's but none was a leader in the KMT (p. 96).

Here is an excerpt from the *General Genealogy of the Wu Clan of Ling-nan*, as compiled by Wu Yao-kuang, a member of the seventy-sixth generation of the clan.

"In the middle of the 17th century the home of our clan was seized by bandits and some of the members moved into the city of T'ai-shan to fight the bandits until the end of the rebellion, and returned later to the village (in 1667). Another branch family in T'ai-shan was spared by the bandits (in 1677) because the household chief was famous as a model of piety. In 1797, the White Lotus rebellion was rampant in Hupeh, Honan, and other provinces. There is also a record of the Wu clan militia network fighting against the Red Turbans around December 1854 during the Taiping Rebellion."

Perhaps it was these disturbances that caused so many of the males of this clan to migrate. Perhaps it was the Taiping Rebellion, which began in 1850 and continued until 1864. Perhaps it was the series of smaller uprisings of secret societies like the Red Turbans, bandit groups, and Triad societies from Canton who created havoc in the Canton Toishan area, the area from which most of the emigration took place. Perhaps it was the famine, food shortages, typhoons, and perhaps it was as is told to us here in American history, the call of the California gold. Whether it was one or all of these reasons, a large number of immigrants from the Canton Toishan area traveled the Pacific, immigrating west to the foreign shores. California was where they first landed. They were from many villages and many clans, but it was the Eng village clan who left California and went East and established Newark Chinatown.

LOOKING FOR CHINATOWN ~ 2

My search for Newark Chinatown continued. I had found that the only records the library had were donated by the Newark Evening News and were only negative reports of raids and the murder in the Mulberry Arcade. So I went to look for the Mulberry Arcade. It was then a patch of land that had a brick paved street, covered over with asphalt, and at that time housed the trucks belonging to the U.S. Postal Service. Who owned the land was another question. I started reading all the materials I found in the Newark Public Library. I could not accept that a whole community of people had lived in this area and all they did was gamble, deal in opium, and shoot each other. Knowing American history and having experienced the Civil Rights Era first hand, I knew there was a lot missing. As I read, I would visit the streets and sights and get a sense of the place that was spoken about.

It was at this time that one day my doorbell rang, and when I answered it, there stood on the step a young man who was looking for work space. He was a Brazilian who had studied Mandarin and developed a love affair with China and all things Chinese. He had seen the sign outside that we ran an art center and was interested in working with us. He had recently returned from China where he had been studying the language and working there. I told him about the Chinatown project; he became very interested and actually spent the next two years helping me with my research. Eduardo Almeida was his name and he had been a student of Betty Sung, the foremost scholar on Chinese history and immigration, and professor emeritus at City College.

Eduardo insisted that we go to her house to speak to her about the project. I did not refuse. Betty Sung lives in one of the very tall apartment buildings built around the '60s and '70s in what is the Confucius Plaza area of New York City Chinatown. She is an amazing woman, about 5-feet 5½ inches, of medium build, with a sweet, pleasant personality. Betty listened to my story about my search for Newark Chinatown, told us about her journey through her scholarship into Chinese history, and sent me to the National Archives with names of people there who would help me. She had, during her research, discovered hundreds of untouched boxes of Chinese immigrant archives in the National Archives vaults. The boxes were falling apart; some were damaged, and all in all they were a mess. Gathering her students, she went about organizing all the materials and documenting them into a software archive that made them accessible to the public and to the families of the people who emigrated from China since the 1800s. Betty Sung was very friendly and pleasant. We had tea and cookies and talked and talked. I examined the books she had written and she recommended books I should read. She gave me information about how and where to begin my research. Her connection at the National Archives gave me total access to all the material, even making copies of the files for me to take with me to do the work. As a matter of fact, very few people ever went to the National Archives then to look up their family histories. Now it is the latest trend. Now we have DNA and we can trace our ancestors back to the cave men.

The official immigration interrogations were amazing. Apparently any Chinese male who traveled back and forth to China was repeatedly interrogated; if his information did not match the records that the Immigration Service had on file, about his city, his family, the number of trees on the street where he lived, he was returned to China. Cheat books were very common and one paid dearly for them. These were memorized completely before one dared venture on the trip to "Gold Mountain."

Betty Sung has, over the years, been very supportive of my efforts, and I have to thank her very much for her constant support and assistance.

At this time I was taking a business course at Seton Hall University. John Richards, then VP of New Jersey Performing Arts

Center, came to the school to speak about the arts in the city of Newark, and my class was required to attend so we could write about his address. I spoke to John and made an appointment to tell him about my project. When he heard about my research into Newark Chinatown, he suggested to the Programs Director, Baraka Sele, that they find funds to assist me with the project. NJPAC, through a grant from the Mellon Fund for Humanities Projects, was the first to fund research into the search for Newark Chinatown. With their backing I was able to get further funds to continue the research, hire interns to assist me, and begin a series of oral histories that would be the backbone of the research. Eduardo Almeida searched court records for deeds and other information as well as assisting me in finding and compiling the research done by Betty Sung on the individuals and families who journeyed from China to America and Newark Chinatown.

PART 2

HOW THE CHINESE GOT TO NEWARK

I

A Brief Look at American History 1850-1862

On July 11, 1846, the American flag was raised at Sutters Fort. California had become American property.

On June 1, 1846, Capt. John A. Sutter and James W. Marshall began the building of a sawmill on American Fork River, California.

On January 24, 1848, gold was discovered at Sutter's mill.

How did this news arrive in China? Did missionaries bring it? Did American ships bringing opium into Hong Kong harbor bring it? No one knows for sure, but the news reached as far east as the shores of Canton and into all the surrounding villages of Guangdong province, including Toishan.

Suddenly everyone believed the stories they were hearing about this "Golden Mountain" or "Gum Shan." Why stay here and suffer? Why stay here where there seemed no future, no way to change the sadness that was their everyday lives? Mothers called their sons and scraped together coins to pay their passage. Husbands sold their wive's jewelry and household goods to raise the passage for the travel. Some borrowed knowing they would have to pay it back or lose their families. Those left behind felt that once the family member who left got there they would send back or return with enough wealth so that those at home could live comfortably and be wealthy too. Of those who arrived in California in the early 1850s, most were interested in finding gold. Chinese men began the long voyage to search for gold.

It was not difficult to get a ship to Golden Mountain; all you needed was a contract or money. The trip across the ocean took months. Very few women came in the company of their husbands. Most young girls were brought for use as prostitutes.

In 1850, 40 ships left Hong Kong for California with thousands of Chinese aboard. By 1852, 25,000 Chinese had reached Gold Mountain. In Sacramento alone the census recorded 804 Chinese males and 10 females. That same year 1852, the Nevada County census recorded 3,396 Chinese. The Gold Rush had been going on for quite some time by the time these Chinese arrived. Some were lucky and found small claims they could work; some returned to Canton with their riches. However, many of the claims the Chinese bought from whites were completely used up or had very little gold left, but due to language difficulties and corruption, there was no way for them to know this until they had been working the claim. The Chinese invented some of the most incredible ways of panning and sifting the smallest amounts of gold from the California ground. They had to be careful too because there were always thieves, ready to steal the little bit they had eked out of the river bed or to sell them a false claim. They found the American West not much different than their own country in the hardship they had to endure, except here they did not have any help from family, the clan or from their friends in the villages. Here, they could not speak the language, and here, they were racially singled out and attacked. They looked different. But there was no turning back, failure was not an option. There were too many people waiting for the results of one's labor. Death was more acceptable than failure.

Once the gold was depleted, the Chinese who had been panning in left over claims of the whites were forced to look for other ways to survive. By 1868 the Chinese could no longer find any prospects in mining. Prior to the discovery of gold, there were less than a hundred Chinese in the West and fewer in the East. These few worked as employees for the rich at low wages. Some had come on their own, some had been brought here by their employers, and some had been bought, sold, or kidnapped to work for wealthy whites.

In 1853 the idea of a transcontinental railroad was an obsession of Theodore Judah, and at the Pacific Railroad Convention of 1859, that dream became a reality. The project was financially masterminded by four ambitious men. They were Collis P. Huntington, Mark Hopkins, Leland Stanford, and Charles Crocker. All were America's self-made success stories of the time. With Judah as the chief engineer and James Strobridge in charge of the construction, the entire project was completed seven years ahead of schedule. Strobridge had been building railroads since the age of 16 and had a reputation for being able to command large groups of men and to bring a project to fruition under adverse circumstances. Mark Hopkins, the treasurer of the organization formed by these four was known for his ability to stay on budget. Huntington was known as a man who would stop at nothing to achieve his goal. Leland Stanford disliked the Chinese and in his 1862 inaugural speech as Governor of Sacramento, he called them "the dregs of Asia," yet at the same time they were building his railroad and far surpassing any of the other workers he could find.

When the railroads began, the idea was to hire only white men; however, as the work progressed and the hardship of the work was apparent, this changed. White railroad workers were not reliable and were not easy to keep. Charles Crocker directed the construction of the Central Pacific Railroad. When he was faced with the problem of finding workers for his railroad project he consulted Strobridge who was familiar with the gold mining crowd and who had mentioned on several occasions the industrious nature of the Chinese miners he had seen, many of whom were now wandering around out of work. He suggested to Leland Stanford that they bring in Chinese to do the work. Stanford and others did not take to the idea claiming that the size and strength of the Chinese would not make them good workers. They also knew that the presence of the Chinese would cause problems with the white workers. They soon found the former to be incorrect. They hired the Chinese at a lower rate than the whites and did not provide room and board. The move was so successful that Crocker decided to bring more Chinese directly from China just for this purpose.

Chinese law prohibited Chinese citizens from immigrating to any other country. For this reason, most Chinese thought of themselves as returning to China after they had acquired their wealth. In July of 1868, the Burlingame Treaty was signed between China and the United States. Created to counteract the Chinese government's prohibition and provide protection from the discrimination, exploitation, and violence Chinese had received at the hands of Americans, the treaty provided that "Chinese subjects visiting or residing in the United States, shall enjoy the same privileges, immunities, and exemptions in respect to travel or residence, as may there be enjoyed by the citizens or subjects of the most favored nation."

Utilizing the legal aspects of the Burlingame Treaty, Crocker contracted with vessels sailing to Canton to bring back Chinese. He estimated he would need about four thousand. Usually passage from China to California was paid for by those Chinese individuals who had raised the funds or by the American contractors, who would then collect the money from the persons hiring the Chinese in San Francisco and who purchased their contracts. This money would be paid back by the worker. Hiring the Chinese saved Crocker money because the Chinese were paid less and their room and board was not provided as it was for white workers. White workers were paid thirty-five dollars per month and were given supplies and meals. Chinese workers made twenty-five dollars per month and paid for their own food, supplies, cook, and headman. For the Chinese, the railroads provided a quick answer to their economic needs and many took it. They lived in tents alongside the railroad line and at one point in the history of the construction actually went on strike for better conditions and were successful.

The United States had sunk money into building railroads not only in the United States but all over the world. The Chinese built railroads not only in the United States but also in Cuba, China, Canada, and just about everywhere there were railroads to be built. They were great at handling dynamite, had little or no fear of heights, and could with the help of their woven baskets lift men onto and out of every mountain peak in which the dynamite was to be placed. Their bravery astonished the non-Chinese workers and so they gained the respect of the other immigrants and non-immigrants who worked alongside them on the railroad lines from West to East.

On May 10, 1869, a crew of eight Chinese men placed the last section of rail. In the photograph commemorating this event, my friend and photographer Corky Lee said he did not see one Chinese worker. This bothered him. Work on the transcontinental railroad had come to an end and suddenly there was no work for thousands of Chinese laborers, who now wandered around the cities of California. A few who had managed to save some of their earnings, and those who were too old to work anymore bought their tickets on steamers back to Canton. Others began their little businesses in the little areas around the cities. Many went to San Francisco Chinatown, some to New York. The American public of the west saw these Chinese s taking their work, and hostility against Chinese which had existed all through the building of the railroads now escalated. By 1870, after a year of being out of work, many Chinese were desperate and ready to go anywhere to work again. The depression of 1873 was later to follow.

By this time there were already two or three generations of Chinese living in the United States. Chinese and Chinese Americans (a term that came later and meant American-born Chinese) spread through the little towns of the West and Midwest and some came East. They started laundries and shops. It was at this time that Charlie King, the first real important leader of Newark Chinatown left San Francisco to go to work in his cousin's laundry in the Midwest. Charlie's story will be detailed later.

In California, the Chinese worked as gardeners and created San Francisco's Chinatown as restaurant workers and merchants. They also started their associations and tongs to help other Chinese and made money from gambling and prostitution. The word *tong* means hall or meeting place. Somehow over the centuries the word became connected with the people gathering in the hall rather than the hall itself. In America we know a *tong* as a Chinese gang, but originally, like the Mafioso, *tongs* were started as organizations or community groups designed and meeting in halls to discuss and create ways to make community laws that helped the community survive. Later on, as communities broke down, these groups evolved into what we now know as the gangs.

12-Ah Sing, Harper's Weekly, July 30, 1870, page 493

II

Ah Sing and the Migration East

Laws in America were different in the nineteenth century. Gambling and prostitution were frowned on by the church, yet accepted by many as part of the social life in early America. In certain areas, American-born first-generation immigrants of English or Irish descent ran most of the town politics. The Italians were just arriving. Here in Newark, the Chinese ran mostly laundries; restaurants came later. The first recorded laundry using Chinese labor is noted in Belleville in 1870, an election year. But the story does not begin in Belleville, New Jersey, but in another state.

In June of 1870, Calvin T. Sampson, a shoe manufacturer in North Adams, Massachusetts, found that his Irish women workers were more than he could tolerate. They had joined the Crispin Union and were being encouraged to strike for better wages and work conditions; two things Sampson felt he could not supply without dipping into his profits.

He refused, determined to fight them. He had heard that the Chinese laborers in San Francisco were a hard working group who could be hired cheaply. So he set out for San Francisco.

While he was away, his workers went on strike. Hearing the news Sampson's resolve became firm. He would remove the workers who were a problem and fill their places with a more acceptable labor force. In California, he saw firsthand the large number of immigrant Chinese workers, now freed from railroad work, who were eagerly soliciting any kind of employment they would be allowed to have. San Francisco's Chinatown was not in existence, but several streets had many Chinese shops. Here Sampson found someone who spoke Cantonese and English and would negotiate for him. This was Ah Sing, a member of the Eng clan. Sampson hired Ah Sing to contract seventy-five Chinese men to come to North Adams to work in the factory. He offered wages, room and board. In California, Chinese workers were being forced to pay a tax of $2.50 a month in order to work. Sometimes $2.50 was a Chinese worker's entire monthly wage, so Sampson's offer of room, board, and wages in the area of eighty dollars per month, without any tax, was heaven.

In a picture of the Chinese immigrants who went to North Adams to work in this factory, I discovered three women. I eagerly examined the women with my magnifying glass to try to identify their racial origin. I was able to positively identify one as Chinese and the others are unknown (see photo on following page). However, since the photo is of Chinese who had come to work at the shoe factory, it is possible that the three women had come to assist or to serve as prostitutes for the men, or perhaps they were the wives of one or more of the men, since Chinese men did marry non-Chinese women. To question the presence of women in this photo was very necessary for me because the history of Chinese women is minimal in the context of early Chinese immigration. Often, any mention of them is within the context of being bought or kidnapped in China and brought here only to serve as prostitutes.

Sampson encountered much resistance from the Crispin Union when he brought his group of Chinese to Massachusetts. However, he found them to be excellent workers who learned the skill of shoe making quite easily, so he was quite happy with them. The news of Sampson's success was widespread and as a result a Belleville businessman named James Hervey, who was in the same predicament, thought he would do the same.

James Hervey was a Scotsman who had made a fortune at sea and had decided to retire on several hundred acres of property he had purchased along the Passaic River. He built a large, extremely beautiful home on a hill overlooking the Passaic River. He opened a steam laundry business on the same property not too far from the house. Hervey was not ready to retire to a sedentary life and saw the laundry as a money making occupation to fill his mental and physical time.

Around this time, factory workers worked long hours and became very dirty from the working conditions that involved the use of coal for steam to run the machines. Unpaved streets and non- existent regular garbage pickup and street cleaning made for very dirty cities as a whole. Laundries were big business and very successful ones at that. Hervey had hired Irish women to work in his laundry and soon he became the brunt of their complaints for higher pay. When Hervey heard of Sampson's success, he contacted him and was given information about Ah Sing. He traveled to California to select Chinese workers for his own use. There he went to meet Ah Sing, who assisted him in recruiting a group of sixty-eight Chinese to return with him to Belleville.

Ah Sing was a unique individual for his time. He was born in a village of Tois-han in Guangdong province. His family was poor and food was scarce, so he was sold to a traveling merchant at the age of ten. Around 1845, sneaking on board a ship from Canton, China, as a boy of thirteen, he was discovered by one of the American sailors and along with being beaten and boxed was put to work emptying and cleaning the chamber pots, scrubbing floors, cleaning various areas of the ship and being the brunt of anyone's abusive behavior. He very soon learned that, in order to survive around Europeans, he had to learn their language and keep his wits tuned. As soon as he was old enough, and with investments from Chinese merchants, he returned to China bringing back goods and women. Within five years, he wrote and spoke English and had worked for every businessman and prostitute in San Francisco, having had several businesses himself. He became a well-known and very influential merchant in the San Francisco Chinese commu-nity, helping to start one of the most famous Chinese Business Associations or Tongs. Ah Sing as a very famous Chinese character, appears in many documents regarding San Francisco's Chinese history. He is noted and mentioned historically as being a very astute businessman, a sneaky, conniving character. But this was the stereotypical way Chinese were mentioned in early history, so we must give some leeway as to what kind of character Ah Sing really was. Corinne Hoexter writes of him in her book *From Canton to California*:

> Norman Ah-Sing or As-Sing the leader of his community in its
> first meetings and celebrations with the white world of San Fran-
> cisco must have been a Chinese attracted to California by the
> lure of gold. In the early 1840's, three hundred of the Chinese
> then in San Francisco elected him a leader of the Chew Yick
> Kung Shaw (Luminous Unity Public Office), the first mutual
> aid society in America. By the end of 1850, Ah Sing had fully
> grasped and utilized California's promise of incredibly speedy
> fortune to the quick-witted, the lucky and the ruthless. (Hoexter,
> Corinne. From Canton to California, The Epic of Chinese Im-
> migration. New York, NY: 1976. pp. 8-9).

Early on, Ah Sing made his riches with a candy store and bakery. Then he moved into the restaurant business, owning two restaurants. His Woosung Restaurant stood on the corner of Kearny and Commercial streets in San Francisco, and there he entertained the local Irish and American politicians and police in enormous ban-quets. He would have been called, by the white San Franciscans, the mayor of Chi-natown, as they did specific merchants like Charles King in Newark Chinatown many years later. But I have a feeling San Francisco had many Chinese like Ah

Sing. Many stories have been written about Ah Sing's life. His love relationship with Atoy has become a well-known romance story. Atoy was a San Francisco Chinese prostitute who ran a brothel and whom Ah Sing tried to destroy when she rejected him, realizing he was also after her businesses. Ah Sing met his match in Atoy.

Since Ah Sing spoke English and was well versed in American culture, his claim to American citizenship was never denied. We have the undeniable fact that he visited Newark and opened a laundry here after assisting to bring the Chinese to the Belleville laundry. For Ah Sing, visiting New Jersey was the same as prospecting for gold; he was looking to see what opportunities he could create for himself.

By the time of the Hervey contract (1870s), Ah Sing's reputation as an extremely profitable Chinese businessman in San Francisco, already dated back to the 1840s. Hervey and Ah Sing met in a restaurant owned by Sing and discussed Hervey's proposition. Ah Sing would get two thousand dollars to find sixty-eight men to go to Belleville to work in the laundry. Funds for their passage as well as other monies were part of the two-year indentureship contract. For Sing this was no problem since he had many of these men arriving from China weekly, as well as those who worked on the railroads and were now out of work. He had already sent seventy-five to North Adams, Massachusettes. These deals were just another profitable business agreement for Ah Sing. He was interested in the idea of profit to be made in laundries in the Eastern part of the United States. He had been hearing stories of a new Chinatown in the East and was curious as to what business deals he could create there. He decided to return to Belleville with Hervey to survey the scene and five years later in downtown Newark funded businesses and a laundry in his name. There are historical documents of a Chinese laundry owned by one Ah Sing which was located on the first floor of what is now the Kislak building, located on the corner of Central Avenue and Broad Street. The brick building of this time is hidden beneath the 1960s façade.

13-Home of James Hervey in Belleville - circa late 1990's, courtesy owner.

III

ARRIVAL IN BELLEVILLE

Most of the men Ah Sing contracted for Belleville were in their teens; the youngest was twelve years old. Charley Sing, a clan cousin, acted as interpreter, treasurer, and foreman. Hervey, aware of the mounting hostility amongst the Irish workers in the country against Chinese immigrants and in Belleville as well, decided to bring in his group in the middle of the night. The Erie Railroad train arrived in Port Jervis on Tuesday morning, September 21, 1870. Hervey arranged for the train to be held up at Port Jervis so that it would arrive in Belleville late into the night. He would send a wagon to pick them up and deliver them back to the laundry. The train however, was even further delayed by sightseers who had never seen so many Chinese persons in one place in their life. Finally at midnight the train pulled into the Belleville station. The station was closed and the wagon driver, thinking the train would not arrive had left the station. As a result the Chinese arrived in Belleville in the wee hours of the morning and had to walk to the laundry. In so doing they were forced to rely on the directions of persons who lived in the area, and thus the residents were made aware of their existence. They finally arrived at the laundry however and were settled in. The next day work began.

The superintendent in charge was named Mr. Van Vorst, with Charley Sing as the foreman. One hundred Irish women were working there at the time. Sixteen stopped work and refused to work with the Chinese. They left but returned at the end of the day asking to be taken back to work. The Chinese received eighty dollars a month in gold, from which they were expected to pay for board and clothing for themselves. Hervey constructed a large wall around the laundry so that passersby could not see what was transpiring on his property. This did not make matters any easier for he had become the brunt of attacks from some of the townspeople and the Crispin Union for replacing Irish workers with the Chinese. Eight days after the arrival of the Chinese, the union activists staged a demonstration across the river from Hervey's house. Hervey's property ran down to the river with the front of the house overlooking it. From across the river on the Belleville side, the Crispin Union shouted their speeches in the direction of the house, adding racial slurs and calling for a return of the Chinese to their homeland.

As upsetting for the family of Hervey as it was, Mrs. Hervey simply closed her windows and shutters overlooking the river and opened the windows on the opposite side of the house, in the direction of the hill on which her husband's laundry lay. Through her living room window she saw the black smoke furiously raging from the laundry chimneys, as the coal burned to create the billowing steam. From the other buildings, she heard the calling of the new Chinese workers in their foreign tongue. She was proud of her husband even though many of the city officials considered him a traitor. The warm fall wind was blowing uphill. *It was a noisy day,* she thought, *just a noisy day.*

From September 22 to November 28, every newspaper in the Belleville, Newark, and New York City area ran the story of the arrival of the Chinese in the East at Hervey's laundry. Some of the newspapers included commentary about the overall "Chinee Question" as they termed their "problem."

The "problem" was the immigration of thousands of Chinese to the United States each year, who were competing for the jobs of the Irish and other immigrants. The "question" was how to stop the importation and immigration of the Chinese. At this time the United States had no immigration laws. People moved freely from Europe and other parts of the world as long as they could afford a ticket. This proved helpful to railroad magnates looking for cheap labor to build their railroads. Although they disliked the Chinese, they were not concerned about the number of Chinese immigrants entering the States since they were looking for cheap labor. But, they were aware of the mounting hostility against them. It wasn't until after the railroads were built that the immigration laws were put in place. On November 6, 1869, the building of the Transcontinental Railroad officially ended. In September of 1870, the Chinese arrived in Belleville; less than a year later, after having finished their indentureship, some had moved to Newark, and in May of 1882, eleven years after their arrival in Newark, the U.S. passed the Chinese Exclusion Laws to stop immigration from China.

14-Norma and See Gat on their wedding day, courtesy Bob Lee.

LOOKING FOR CHINATOWN ~ 3

My days of hunting included spending time going through every page of the Newark Evening News for one hundred years, an eye-excruciating experience and a costly one, since I made a copy of every article that concerned Newark Chinatown and some that showed the temperament of the people of the day towards the Chinese population.

I photographed all the properties that I discovered to be Chinese owned and built. I traveled wherever it was necessary and made lots of friends and discovered so much about my own Chinese history. One day I visited Old First Presbyterian Church and asked to examine their records. I was refused, but was able to convince them to give me a few names and addresses of some of the Chinese congregation, past and present. I then sent out letters to all of these people telling them about the project and how important it was for me to meet and interview them and get their history. At the top of my list was the name Philip Eng Wong. I never got a response from Philip, but soon I was told that I needed to speak to his mother, Norma Eng Wong, who was the real power of Newark Chinatown. I sent out a letter to Norma telling her about my research and asking if I could interview her. I received no answer. I got her phone number from a member of the Chinese community. By now word had gotten around the community that I was doing the research and people were curious and slightly thrilled. Norma refused to see me for about a year and a half. I had called the house several times, each time speaking to her son Paul. He would say "I will ask her," and I would get no response, but finally one day I called and got a "Yes." I was thrilled, and ecstatic. I took my binders of photos, the information I had collected, and my tape recorder, and on the evening of my appointment I drove up to South Orange. It was a simple house, one you would pass unnoticed. I parked my car and went up the few stairs and rang the doorbell. Paul's wife, Janet, answered the door and invited me in, introducing herself. I met Paul, their son Christopher, Norma Eng and George and May Eng, and their neighbors and relatives. We all sat down on the sofa, and I pulled out my tape recorder and placed it in a central position, opened my binder with the photos of the raids I had found at the Newark Public Library, and began my story.

Norma Eng Wong
When I first started the project, the folks at the Old First Presbyterian Church expressly cited Norma Eng Wong as a very important person with whom to speak. I couldn't conjure up her image but I had heard enough about her that I could feel her presence when I spoke on the phone to other members of her family. After several of these calls, with background conversations that I couldn't make out, I had begun to imagine a picture of a regal elderly Chinese empress dowager in traditional Chinese clothes sitting in a chair presiding over her family. Boy was I wrong. As I began to interview more and more people, I got a totally different picture of Norma Eng Wong. Everyone I spoke to, elders and several members of the younger generation stated the admiration they had for her and the difference she made in their lives. They said she had delivered Newark Chinatown babies, cared for them and knew them all by name. By now I had begun to fall in love with Norma Eng Wong; she began to be my heroine. One day, Frank Eng invited me to lunch with Paul, and the ice was broken. Then, a year before I met her, I found a newspaper photo of her in a 1955 newspaper, holding her son Paul, who was being christened, but the picture was very grainy and unclear. Now that I was finally face to face with Norma, I marveled at her vivacious energy and her exceptional memory for details. The interview lasted two to three hours and we were mentally exhausted when it was all over. But I knew that my thoughts were correct. This was the star of any book, movie, or presentation I would make on Newark Chinatown.

Petite is not the word for Norma Eng Wong; tiny is a better word, but her aura is so large that you have to remind yourself that you are really looking at a very small woman. I would visit her at her house and we would sit for hours around her kitchen table talking. We met more and more often until we saw each other about once a week, when she was not in California visiting her daughter. One day when I went to visit her, she was making sticky rice. "My daughter loves sticky rice and insists that I make it and bring it when I come to visit her," she said to me. So here was this tiny 80-plus-year-old Chinese woman standing at the kitchen table with a huge pot, wrapping rice and sausages and other meats into a palm leaf and folding it neatly, tying it with a string. Before I knew it she was teaching me how to fill, wrap, and tie Nuomi Fan. We worked at this, talking for hours until we filled the huge pot.

March 16, 2002 – Diary Entry:
At this writing Norma is in California visiting her daughter. I worry about her because she has cancer and every day I say a prayer that she could live longer. I pray that I can spend some more time with her. A selfish thought, but all her family prays for this too, and she is now family to me. Norma is such a feisty woman that one morning I went to visit her and she said to me, "I stopped taking my medicine. I told the doctor it was making me feel so sick that it couldn't be doing me any good. So I stopped taking it," she said "and now I feel much better." "When did you stop," I asked? "Last week," she replied, and I remembered that the last time I spoke to her she wasn't able to go anywhere.

I am waiting for her to come back from California so we can continue our visits. The day before she left we had breakfast in a coffee shop on South Orange Avenue in South Orange. She was her spunky self, looking forward to the visit with her daughter and seeing her friends in California. Perhaps California is the second home of every Chinese person of her generation. She started telling me about her father and how he would come to visit her as a child and she stated, "I loved him because he played with me. I remember he used to play with me, and when you're a child that is very important, so you always remember those memories." I listened as she spoke about her young life in Chinatown, NY, growing up on Doyer's Street.

The summer of 2002 was not a good one for Norma. Had I
known that day, as we sat drinking coffee and reminiscing, that
I would lose her so soon, I would have taken more photographs
of her and taped more of our conversations instead of just en-
joying her company as much as I did. In order to be a good jour-
nalist one must always be objective, uninvolved, and constantly
aware of your project. It was hard to do this with Norma. Somehow she wanted you to be a part of her and you wanted to be a
part of her, so you couldn't hold yourself back to think about
her as a project and be photographing all the time because her
presence was so great to be around. You wanted to listen and
feel her energy and watch her eyes as she spoke, and her cheeks
and skin and the smile she gave with each memory and how
could you savor these things with your eye behind a camera. It
just wasn't possible. Now I have lost those things forever to my
camera, but I carry them in my memory. Norma returned from
California sometime around the beginning of the summer. I
don't know how she fared in San Francisco because she never
dwelt on her sickness. I did know that she returned and was too
ill to see me on several occasions that I had called. I sent her
flowers, spoke to her on the phone and could tell she was tired
because we never spoke long. When I asked to see her she was
not well enough. It was apparent that she was dying and I respectfully stayed away. The week before she passed, I called and
was told that she had turned for the worst. Then I got a call from
Janet that she had passed. I miss her very much. We had some
wonderful times together.

Paul Eng Wong, Norma's youngest son, read the eulogy.
I would like to take this opportunity to thank you all for coming
today and to say a few words about my mother, Norma. Norma
Wong was a unique woman who inspired everyone around her.
Her sincerity, warmth, and smile could make strangers feel like
old friends and old friends feel like special loved ones. She also
could always see the good in people. Which is why, I think, she
loved life and the many wonderful people who she met along
the way.

She often said that throughout her life God had blessed her
by sending her guardian angels to protect her and her family in
her greatest times of need. I would now like to thank all these

people: Grandpa and Grandma Chow - who played a role in raising her and her brother. Uncle David - who protected and cared
for her and has been a life-long friend. Daniel Leong - her
younger brother whom she loved dearly. Marie "Grandma"
Banta - who taught her about Jesus and gave her hope. Aunt
Jeanyee and Uncle Wai - who gave us kids many hours of joy
while she worked. Arlene and Orlando Bell - who saved Mom
from despair when Dad was very ill. Russell Sherrow – who
watched over us and became our Uncle Russell. My brother, sisters, and I would like to thank Christopher, Mom's eldest grand-
child, for watching over her and sharing a special bond with her.
This was one of Mom's great joys.

My family has been blessed with countless stories of
Norma's remarkable life and now I'd like share some of them
with you. Mom was born in Detroit, then raised in San Francisco
and New York City. In 1943 she married my Dad and moved to
Newark where they operated the Shanghai Restaurant for twenty
years. I have many fond memories of those times. I also remember how hard my Mom worked at the restaurant to provide for
all of us. I will be forever grateful to my Mom for all her years
of sacrifice and toil.

It was in Newark that Mom became involved with the Old
First Church. She was a devoted Christian and was very active
in the Church. Mom loved all the people at Old First. She made
it a point to greet each of them every time she was there. There
is one person who really stands out in our hearts and that is Betty
Anderson, our children call her Grandma A. It was in those years
at Old First that Mom instilled the importance of God and spir-
ituality to her children.

In 1963, after a few stints with temporary jobs, she decided
to participate in a pilot program for the new hospital position of
Unit Manager at St. Michael's Hospital. Mom became one of
the first people to be trained and certified in this new position.
She worked tirelessly at St. Michael's for twenty-three years.
During this time she instituted many innovative procedures to
improve the operations in Center 2. She also made many friends
at the hospital. Two of them, Mary Ellen and Maureen, have remained life-long friends. Mom retired in 1985 and moved to the
hills of Sussex County with my brother Phil. In 1990 Mom
moved to South Orange and lived with my family and me. This

opened another chapter in her life. She made friends with the women at the "Club." She loved going to the Baird Center, sitting by the duck pond, playing Bocce Ball, going on trips to the mall or longer trips down the shore. She loved you all and enjoyed your company immensely. Her calendar was so filled with activities that it was often difficult to remember where she was going next. One of her dearest friends, Vera, passed away a couple of weeks ago and now they are together again.

Mom also loved to travel and was a familiar face at ITE venues. ITE is a professional engineering society that I belong to. When I attended various conferences, my family, including Mom, often accompanied me. Once again Mom made many friends and was loved by many at ITE. She would often reminisce the times and places we visited and she took great pleasure in watching television and recognizing places where she'd been. She also traveled to the West Coast often to visit my sisters and enjoyed the sites in California and Hawaii. Some of her friends at the Baird called her the gypsy because she traveled so much. As many of you know, we have an extended family on my dad's side. My older brothers and sister and their families have always been an important part of Mom's life. We want to thank Dai Gaw, Dai So, Sam Gaw, Sam So, Eng Gaw, Eng So, King Fung and her husband, and all of our nieces and nephews for their love and respect for Mom. During the past few weeks my brothers and their families visited Mom and brought her favorite foods and comforted her. I want to thank my niece Betty for making this possible. Mom once told me that when she passes on and people ask about her, tell them that I went away on a long vacation. I think that she said that because she didn't want her friends and family to feel badly about her passing. That's the way Mom lived her life, always thinking of others. We are all here not to mourn her death but to celebrate her life and to rejoice in her entering the Kingdom of God. Thanks, Mom, for all you've done for us. We know that you will always be with us in our hearts and our minds and we will love and remember you always.

No one cried that day— at least no one I saw—but no one looked really happy either. People greeted each other forming groups to talk awhile then moving on to another group and so forth. The funeral was the following morning, but I couldn't bring myself to go. Ever since I was five, when my grandfather was buried, I never could watch the casket going into the ground and being covered with dirt.

When I was a little girl, my hero was Joan of Arc. She was the only woman warrior I had ever heard of. Then when I came to America I discovered Wonder Woman and then Katy Keene. As a young woman in art school I lived on Delancey Street in what is now part of Chinatown. I discovered the Jade Palace Theatre and all the woman warriors of the traditional Chinese historical classics. My favorite actress was Ivy Ling Po. The movies had subtitles and the screen was very big for the time. Sometimes the theatre was packed other times it was sparse. I read the subtitles and practiced saying the words in Chinese in my mind as I watched and noticed body language, formal movements and of course the martial arts. I should have taken a course in Chinese then but my life was so complex as a single parent that I could think of nothing but getting to work to make the next dollar. My daughter sat hunched down in the seat next to me in the dark, and sometimes we took her friend Zack with us. He lived in the loft next door. When I could afford it we had popcorn too, but most of the times we just came to see the movie. These were the first and only movies my daughter ever saw as a child. Chinatown movies were cheap and they were very exciting, and they were Chinese.

PART 3

THE BALDWINS & THE FIRST CHINESE NEW YEAR

15- Isaac Baldwin member of the Baldwin Family, circa 1800's, courtesy NJ Historical Society

I

THE BALDWINS, 1666 TO 1950S

The families of Baldwins, Cranes (family of Stephen Crane, Civil War author), and Seymours (all early New Jersey settlers) were the first to inadvertently assist with the move of the Chinese to Newark's Mulberry Street area and the creation of a Newark Chinatown. I asked myself why these people would want to aid Chinese immigrants and found the answer in looking into their personal philosophy, their religious views, and their lives.

The city of Newark was founded by a group of English settlers who fled religious persecution in England. They had originally settled outside the jurisdiction of English law in Milford, now part of the state of Connecticut. When English governance extended to Milford, they again migrated. Under the leadership of Reverend Abraham Pierson, a man with strict ideas on religion and government, they left Milford and struck out on their own. The group moved from one area to another in their search, despite the hardships involved each time in clearing new land, farming, hunting for food and bearing families. Finally they settled in this area and named it Newark. The first group arrived here in a small band in 1666 and the second in the spring of 1667.

Among the second group of families to arrive were two members of the Baldwin family, John Baldwin Senior and John Baldwin Junior. They received parcels of land in what we now know as the Mulberry, McCarter, and Hamilton Street area of downtown Newark. The land remained in the family for two hundred and ninety years. The Baldwin homestead was torn down around 1900 to build a fire station for the area. The last Baldwin family members, two sisters, died in the 1950s in the family town house around the corner from the Lafayette Street fire station. The house was at 77 Lafayette Street and was destroyed in 2006 to make room for the

Prudential Arena. It was a beautiful three-story red brick building with brick-brack design under the bay windows and at the top of the building.

In the 1800s, Newark had an annual directory of its residents. At that time, the Baldwin family had already spread to different parts of the state, but 150 were recorded still living in Newark and carrying the name Baldwin. There were also offspring who through intermarriage were Baldwins, but did not carry the Baldwin last name. The families were apparently very religious and of varying Protestant faiths. Some were Methodist, some were Presbyterian, and others belonged to the many denominations existing in Newark. One of the founders of the First Baptist Peddie Memorial Church was Kipps Baldwin.

For generations there were quite a few Baldwins who were known for their missionary zeal, traveling abroad to India and China. In the January 17, 1898, edition of *The Newark Evening News,* there is an article about two Baldwin sisters preparing to leave on a missionary journey to the South Pacific. The article also mentions other Baldwin family members who had left for Turkey. According to an article by Murray A. Rubenstein entitled *The Wars They Wanted: American Missionaries' Use of the Chinese Repository before the Opium War*, the social situation of America in the 1840s was a time when young men were pulled into a missionary zeal, entering religious colleges to become career evangelists. Rubenstein claimed that the changing economic conditions and job insecurity led to situations where young middle class men could not find jobs in their field and did not wish to work in their father's business. With the redefinition of the role of the minister they became easily drawn into evangelical pursuits among the "heathens" abroad.

Missionary work was a paid job with room and board and the excitement of travel to foreign lands. There was also the conviction that saving "the Heathen" was the only way to save the world. And saving the world meant saving the American economic situation (opening China to trade), bringing about the great day of religious awakening and economic prosperity as predicted in the Bible. Young men and women of the Protestant faith, according to Rubenstein, set out to open China to world availability. The world at the time was experiencing the Western nations of England, the United States, and France involved in a second stage of world colonization, the first stage beginning with Columbus' "discovery of the New World."

II

THE MISSION IN CHINA

On September 30, 1847, two Methodist missionaries arrived in Fuzhou (also known as Foochow), China. The Methodist Board had been, since 1835, wanting to start missions in China. After several studies on the subject, Fuzhou was chosen, money was raised, and a small group was sent off. Under the treaty of Nanking, signed between Britain and China, Fuzhou was one of five Chinese ports opened up to trade. It was a large city of about 500,000 inhabitants and had had some experience with Catholic missionaries in the seventeenth century. In the eighteenth century, because of severe persecution, the Catholics left the area. Between 1844 and 1854 the city experienced a rapid growth in foreign trade.

By 1850, there were three missionary groups in Fuzhou: the American Board of Commissioners for Foreign Missions, whose roots were in the old Congregational churches in New England; the Board of Foreign Missions of the Methodist Episcopal Church; and the Church Missionary Society, whose connections were to the Church of England and the Church of Ireland.

In his book entitled *The Foochow Missionaries 1847-1880* (on page 3), Ellsworth C. Carlson, describes Fuzhou as a Chinese administrative center, which served as the provincial capital as well as the headquarters of the governor-general of Fukien and Chekiang. The city was also a traditional center of learning. It was the site of the annual examinations for the first *hsiu-ts'ai* degree, held twice in five years, and the second *chu-jen* degree. These were extremely difficult exams. The *hsiu-ts'ai* degree was the equivalent of the British B.A., with 20,000 candidates taking the exam and approximately 100 passing. The *chu-jen* was the equivalent of an M.A. and had 60,000 applicants with approximately 300 passing. The *chin-shih,* the final examination, equivalent to a PhD, was the highest academic degree.

Each degree entitled the owner to a specific post in the hierarchy of government, along with which came a specific government sum.

Within the walled city, large numbers of men of property and learning resided. The Westerners referred to these as the "literati" or the "gentry." Ellsworth describes the history of missionary work in Fuzhou as "the story of interaction between representatives of Western religion and culture, on the one hand, and a thoroughly Chinese environment on the other."

China in the nineteenth century was under pressures of great economic constraints. The major causes of these were from natural disasters, demographic relations of the various clans and peoples in the villages, the administrative pressures of the Manchus, and the excessive rents, taxation, and political corruption that existed within village society. Most Chinese in this period existed within a slender margin above subsistence level.

The Americans in Fuzhou found life in China extremely difficult. They were surrounded by constant illness and death among their peers as well as among the Chinese population. Their persistence was rationalized by their consuming faith in their own superiority over other "lesser peoples." This rationalization, under the guise of religion, provided amazing stamina. Among the first group to arrive was a young man who had studied medicine but was not a doctor. The Board of Foreign Missions had not seen the necessity to send a doctor, since they were interested in saving souls not lives. The young man, however, soon found himself saving the lives of men, women, and children. He found that opium poisoning was one of the most prevalent causes of deaths among the Chinese because it was taken as a means of committing suicide.

The first doctor was not sent to Fuzhou until July 9, 1851, four years after the first group of missionaries arrived. During this early conversion period, there were reports of several members of the missionary crew who had differences of opinion as to the role of the missionary settlement in China. Some expressed their realization of what they felt was the absurdity of the evangelical task in relation to the reality of daily life in China and the true needs of the Chinese people. Some tried to make changes, but eventually they resigned their posts and left.

On February 28, 1848, the first missionary school for boys was opened. Later, schools for girls were also created. The schools served as a place where the many urchins who ran freely through the streets could be picked up by the missionaries and harnessed into a working group of helpers. The schools also brought the missionaries into direct contact with parents, who saw them as a place for their children to be fed, clothed, and cared for when they could not do these things themselves. The success of the schools was the most beneficial aspect of missionary zeal. The children learned to read and write in Chinese as well as English, and as they proved their ability and progressed to adulthood, many were given a miniscule salary for their work at the missionary center. The schools for girls became so successful that the wealthy class sent their daughters to be taught the classics of English and Chinese literature. These schools eventually led the fight against foot binding. The schools initiated friendly contact with the parents of the children and the leaders of the town, breaking down prejudices and doubts, and eliciting praise from the "literati" and "gentry," creating that much needed good will so important for the missionaries to continue their business.

One of the reasons the American Missionary Board chose Fuzhou was because of its reputation for having excellent printing facilities which allowed for mass printing of religious information for dissemination to the Chinese public. In 1853 and 1854, the Taiping Rebellion seriously interrupted missionary activities, but Fuzhou escaped attack. By February 1854, as a result of disease, only two missionaries remained in Fuzhou. The Methodist Board in the United States pulled together generous contributions and began soliciting new blood to strengthen the Fuzhou mission. The first Chinese convert was baptized in Fuzhou on July 14, 1857. On October 18 of the same year, six more converts were baptized; by this time, the social gatherings for prayer services had become fully developed in Fuzhou. Sunday school included a "love feast" which was attended by all the Church members and any other interested Chinese. At every love feast, tea and sesame cakes were served. For many Chinese, this was a day's meal or a supplement to it.

The year 1858 saw one of the largest recruitments of Americans to Fuzhou, to date. It was at this time that Stephen L. Baldwin, recently graduated from Concord Biblical Institute and a member of the Newark Conference, was inducted. Stephen Baldwin's father had run a printing press in which Stephen had worked as a young boy before going off to missionary school. One may wonder what could have possessed this young man to give up working in his father's printing business, and eventually taking over the successful enterprise, to venture out into unknown territory and forge a life for himself among the "Heathen Chinee." Stephen appears to have been a very strong-willed and ambitious young man who saw this as an opportunity to make a path to fame. He loved to write and well into his later years wrote for *The New York Times* and other publications. He was a leader and knew he came from an inherited line of established community leaders. He saw a role for himself in the changing times and was determined to fulfill his destiny at any cost.

Because all missionaries had to be married and accompanied by their wives, Stephen became friendly with the young nineteen-year-old Helen Goorham, whose father was a reverend in the church. In September 1858, they were married. That year Stephen and his young wife sailed for Fuzhou. The Fuzhou mission continued to have devastating results on the health of American men and women. Not long after the arrival of the Baldwins in China, Mrs. Baldwin developed a serious chronic disorder. Over the next year, Helen's health became worse. Stephen, realizing that he was at the beginning of his career, felt that at this time he could not return to America with his wife. Helen did not wish to travel alone or leave Stephen behind, so they traveled to Hong Kong to seek professional medical advice. Since medical costs were not included in missionary salaries, Stephen could not afford the care for his wife in Hong Kong and asked for an advance. They remained in Hong Kong for several months, but after Helen's intense suffering, the couple embarked from Hong Kong for America with the hope of saving her life. The delay had taken its toll. On March 16, 1861, Mrs. Baldwin died at sea at the age of twenty-one. Baldwin promptly returned to the mission. The following year he married Esther E. Jerman, a young woman with ambitious desires for her career as the wife of an evangelist. She was, for her time, an independent-minded and intelligent woman who loved to write.

By 1865, of the small group of missionaries, three couples only were left. One of these was the Baldwins. Stephen Baldwin and his new wife were a strong guiding force in the Fuzhou missionary. They and their colleagues decided they had to alleviate the shortage of staff. The Fuzhou mission began not only converting and baptizing more Chinese but also allowing the Chinese to hold positions of responsibility in the organization. In 1869, seven Chinese were ordained to deacon's orders and four were immediately raised to elders. By 1873, Stephen Baldwin was appointed to Superintendent of the Fuzhou mission.

16- Chinese Celebrating New Year at Hervey's Laundry, Leslies Illustrated, 11 March 1871 courtesy NJ Historical Society

17- Chinese Celebrating New Year at Hervey's Laundry Leslies Illustrated, 11 March 1871, courtesy NJ Historical Society

III

THE BALDWINS AND
THE FOUNDING OF NEWARK CHINATOWN

In the fall of 1870, Stephen and his wife Esther returned to Newark to raise monies for further missionary work. On their arrival home, the Baldwins came face to face with the Belleville laundry incident. Immediately, their missionary experience went into high gear. They set about to prove to the general public that the Chinese were not only people of good character, intelligent, and with good moral intentions, but that they were also eager converts to the Christian faith and the Christian way of life.

They went to Hervey's estate and began the conversion of Chinese workers there. Esther went to the nearest church in the area of the Belleville laundry (the Dutch Reformed Church) that would accept her offer and arranged to organize Sunday schools for the Chinese to receive education in Christian doctrine and to learn English along with Western customs.

Stephen Baldwin set about writing several articles that appeared daily in the *Newark Evening News.* In these articles he spelled out the virtues of the Chinese, giving examples from his missionary experience. He delivered several lectures at Halsey Street Methodist Episcopal Church of Newark.

Esther Baldwin had started the publication of a magazine in Fuzhou called *The Heathen Woman's Friend.* In Newark, she wrote several pamphlets which she and Stephen dispersed to the public, pointing out that although the Chinese were heathens, they did have many outstanding qualities, some of which Westerners could learn from.

Through her efforts, the Chinese at the Belleville laundry were able to celebrate Chinese New Year in the traditional way. The Baldwins were very instrumental in promoting the celebration and invited their wealthy contacts to partake of the event.

Food, drink, musical instruments, firecrackers, and ornamental decorative items were part of the celebration. The event was publicized as a way for the public to meet and see that the "Heathen Chinese" could be civilized and also to familiarize Westerners with some modicum of Chinese culture. The response was successful. The event was well attended and in the coming years became an event much looked forward to by people in the neighboring and surrounding communities.

There were three other families involved in the lives of the Chinese during their 100 year sojourn in Newark. They were the Cranes, Crowells, and Seymours. The Crane family was the family of Stephen Crane who wrote the famous novel *The Red Badge of Courage.* These groups of families provided the support system that allowed the Chinese to create the "Chinatown" in the Mulberry and Lafayette Street area, behind City Hall. The Baldwins and Cranes owned most of the property in this area, going back to the late 1700s. The Crowells and Seymours came later. By the 1800s, the Baldwin and Crane and early settler families had multiplied eight generations. Their residences and town houses were on the properties that had once been their farms. They knew who had rooms and store fronts for rent, and being a religious "God fearing" family and outstanding members of the community, they had a say in what happened in the community around Mulberry Street, Lafayette Street (at that time called Fair Street), and Green Street, very close to Broad and Market, the center of town.

With the widespread depression that followed the Civil War, houses were either being sold or rented out as rooming houses to European immigrants employed in the industries that filled the area. Entire floors of brownstones became rooming houses for Chinese men.

One of the Baldwin houses at 81 Lafayette, which I owned, and where I lived in 2000, was one of these homes. The house was a red brick, three-story, one-family home; simple in design, with beautiful carved wooden fireplaces. In the basement there was a coal chute and a huge brick cooking fireplace, reset deeply into the wall with a chimney leading to the roof. The original Baldwin homestead well was in the backyard, with an apple tree and an old iron fence separating the garden from the house. The well has been documented as a place for storytelling by an old African-American slave of the Baldwins. The second floor and third floor were the original bedrooms of the house. These became the rooms that Chinese men rented from the Baldwin families. The bathtub on the second floor was a large old claw-footed, cast iron, white enameled bath, near a window overlooking the backyard. The building to the left was the main Baldwin house that replaced the homestead; this also became a rooming house on the second and third floor. Usually the first floor was maintained by the owner, but in some cases even these were rented out to boarders.

Each room held two or three small cots, and each man had a space of his own. In some of the flats, one group occupied the beds in the day and a different crew came in at night. Many either worked in restaurants or in the laundries in the neighborhood. Sometimes the flats were rented out by the laundry or restaurant owners specifically for the workers to have a place to sleep. During the 1970s, I worked for a Chinese restaurant that owned a small house next door to the restaurant, which housed many new immigrant male workers, some of whom may have been illegal, but who worked long hours at the restaurant.

By the 1890s, the land around these town houses were further developed as downtown Newark became an industrial hub. As the connection with New York Chinatown grew, Chinese, including Charles King, began to open restaurants, grocery shops, and other places of business; not only in the Mulberry Street area, but in the general downtown area, and surrounding areas. Until the 1800s, the city properties had changed hands only among family members. As the nineteenth century drew to a close, bringing railroads, trolley lines, and automobiles, many of the homes in the Lafayette and Mulberry area were rented or bought by Chinese, a few Irish or Germans. Unlike the Irish, Germans, or Italians however, few Chinese of that time considered acquiring the American dream. They all wanted to return to their homeland and retire. The money they had made on Golden Mountain would have allowed them and their families to live in China in relative comfort, if not wealth.

During their sojourn on Golden Mountain, most sent money back home whenever they could, and every man's dream was to return home. The unreality of this became more evident as the hardships of the work, the economic situation, and the exclusion laws set in. Those who did not make it back home hoped that at some point a family member or friend would gather their bones to return them to the family plot so their souls could rest in peace. This, however, was not always the case. As I have mentioned, many of the men who worked in the Belleville laundry were buried in the basement of the Dutch Reformed Church in Belleville. There was some hope that sometime in the future their bones would be taken back to China to their ancestral graves. Unlike the Westerners, burial for the Chinese was no simple situation, and there were the responsibilities of the living to the dead person after the person was buried.

The Baldwin house became my home in 1995. My husband and I bought it with our pension savings. It had been broken into three apartments at that time, one on each floor, and was owned by a Chinese family who also owned a restaurant on Halsey Street. The restaurant became a fish market in the sixties and, having gone s, is still there as a buffet lunch restaurant today. My daughter he third floor, which was originally the maid's quarters. The second floor were converted into a two-bedroom apartment ree bedroom by removing the walk-in closets, which were ... room. I found all manner of paraphernalia under the floor boards, including Chinese calendars and a picture of a young Chinese man in a suit, probably taken to send home to China. It could have been turn of the century but it had a New Brunswick stamp on the back, as the address of the photographer. It was wrapped in a small child's pillow stuffed in a hole in the back of a closet. In the basement, there were dishes, some dating back to the 1960s and some earlier, dark brown medicine containers which were used to steep herbs, wooden boxes from the 30s and 40s, and old silverware with the early plastic handles I remember from my childhood. These items I saved and became attached to as mementos of a time gone forever. As I stood in the house, whether it was the basement or the first or second floor, the voices of the past engulfed me. Feelings and memories of people and children played in my mind and I could sense their movements in and around the rooms. I loved that house. It was the first thing I had ever owned.

Sometime in the 1950s, the last Baldwin to live in the area died in the house next door at 77 Lafayette Street, right behind the fire station that faced into Mulberry Street where the original Baldwin homestead had stood for over a century. Frank Eng remembered it and told me about it. She was an unmarried woman who had lived there with her brother who died earlier. Frank said she had been dead for quite a while before they found her body. I used to imagine a tall thin woman standing by the long window of the smooth, red brick, three-story house with the cut brick-brack design below the window sill, peering through the lace curtains, looking out on the world that had changed so many times around her until she had become totally invisible, so much so that no one remembered that she was there and no one missed her until she had been gone from this world for quite a while. I tracked down the Baldwin family and found the descendent of the last Baldwin of that time living in Brooklyn. He had been a writer for *The New York Times*. I left several messages on his phone but never got a call back. I imagined he was possibly an old man who did not want to be bothered so I gave up.

18-A Chinese laundry in my native country still run as it was generations ago, 2004, courtesy the author.

19-Brown bagged clothes in Peter Moy laundry Trinidad, 2004, courtesy the author.

Looking for Chinatown - 4

Remembering a Chinese Laundry

The first Chinese laundry I remember was in my home country of Trinidad. Laundries were for single workingmen of another class than we were, or for white British families. Most everyone in my town, whom I knew, did their laundry in tubs in the back-yard, hung the wet laundry on rope lines in the yard, or laid the mostly white pieces of clothing out on a bed of large rocks to bleach in the sun. They were later ironed by hand on tables cov-ered with folded sheets. If ironing boards existed, no one had them and I had never seen one. The iron was heated on coal pots which were Y-shaped and made of heavy black cast iron with metal handles. Coal was placed in the lower half of the Y and the iron sat on a metal grating that lay in the neck. These cooking pots were also used for cooking food. The Chinese laundries I knew were no different; they just took in other people's wash and had more clothes lines and more irons. But originally all the washing and ironing was done in someone's yard. I remember peeking through a hole in a neighborhood fence to look at the back yard of one of the laundries with its many lines of clothes blowing in the warm tropical breeze or sunning on the bleach of stones to whiten. Starch was different than we know it now. At that time it was a powdered mass to which water was added and stirred and stirred, then cooked to a white pasty clear sauce that was made into a thinner soupy mess in differing consistencies, depending on how stiff the customer wanted his clothing. The clothing was then rinsed in this soup and hung out to dry. We never sent my father's clothes to the laundry; we never could afford it. My mother washed and ironed them herself.

The Chinese laundry shops were usually small shops where the owners lived in the back. In the shop area were shelves with rows and rows of the clean clothing wrapped in brown paper squares. Some stores had a white ticket attached to each bundle; smaller stores had a name scribbled in soft pencil on the brown paper.

Brown paper was what everything you bought was wrapped in, from a quarter pound of butter to a half pound of rice, and there was a special way of folding the brown paper around the item and tucking it in just right. No tape was used and the package never fell apart. My mother always saved the brown paper. She could use it for anything, and since white paper was costly, the brown paper took its place. She used it to teach us how to write, she used it to write notes to other family members, she used it for grocery lists that I took to the grocer, and she used it to teach us how to make the paper flowers she would sell at Christmas time to get money to buy us toys. She used it for everything. Brown paper became such a special item in my collective unconscious, that later when I lived on the Lower East Side of Manhattan raising my daughter, I would take my white summer pants to the Chinese laundry on Third Street and First Avenue just so they could be nicely pressed and starched and wrapped in brown paper. Like my mother, I also saved the brown paper.

I returned to Trinidad in 2004 to work on another Chinese History Project there and went looking for Chinese laundries. There were still several of the old-style Chinese hand laundries in downtown areas. The difference was that now more of the families had integrated racially. But what hadn't changed was that while the grand folks ran the laundry, the grandkids ran around the shop playing tag. And on the shelf still stood the packages of clothing, wrapped in brown paper. For me, this was home.

Robert Lee 's Memories of His Father's Laundry in Newark Chinatown

It was Bob Lee who introduced to me the idea of the existence of Newark Chinatown, and to whom I went for answers, and it

Form 430   APPLICATION OF ALLEGED AMERICAN CITIZEN OF THE CHINESE RACE FOR PREINVESTIGATION OF STATUS   TRIPLICATE

NO. 139/16
New York (Chinese)

U. S. DEPARTMENT OF LABOR
IMMIGRATION SERVICE

New York, N. Y.

Commissioner of Immigration
and Naturalization,   October 6 , 1934.

To   *Officer in Charge, Immigration Service,*

Ellis Island, N.Y.H., N.Y.

SIR: It being my intention to leave the United States on a temporary visit abroad, departing and returning through the Chinese

Age 18OR   Height 5 ft. 3½ in.
(In shoes)

port of entry of Seattle, Washington , I hereby apply, under the provisions of Rule 16 of the Chinese Regulations, for preinvestigation of my claimed status as an American citizen, submitting herewith such documentary proofs (if any) as I possess, and agreeing to appear at such time and place as you may designate, and to produce then and there witnesses for oral examination regarding the claim made by me.

Marks Scar bridge of nose between eyes; scar rt. cheek at nostril.

This application is submitted in triplicate with my photograph attached to each copy, as required by said rule.

Respectfully,

Signature in Chinese 簽 唐 字 名 李福堂

Signature in English 簽 番 字 名 *Lee Fook Hong*

Address 具 禀 人 之 住 址 C/o H.R. Sisson, 11 Moore St.
New York City

相 簽 詢 委 亦 憑 國 九 而 棸 又 遊 欲 委 管
三 名 問 員 親 據 出 歟 回 亦 出 外 暫 員 理
幅 禀 口 之 與 呈 世 之 茲 卽 埠 入 邦 離 知 外
上 供 公 證 上 所 例 依 由 而 之 今 美 之 人
並 照 辦 人 查 有 在 三 該 去 港 由 國 我 入
附 例 房 到 驗 之 美 十 埠 將 華 出 現 口

OFFICE OF

, 19

Respectfully returned to

Commissioner of Immigration,
Inspector in Charge.

with the information that I have the application on the basis of the evidence submitted herewith.

1t—73   GOVERNMENT PRINTING OFFICE

Commissioner of Immigration,
Inspector in Charge.

20- Bob Lee's Father's Interrogation Papers to enter US dated 1934, courtesy National Archives.

was with Bob Lee with whom I had discussions from the beginning about what Newark Chinatown was all about, and still today we sit and ponder and discuss.

November 7, 2002
Interview with Robert Lee, Director at the Asian American Art Center
Interview was held at AAAC on Bowery, in NYC Chinatown.

Yoland   This is November 7. We are at the Asian American Art Center with Bob Lee, who was born in Newark Chinatown.

Yoland   Bob, I want to start with where you were born. What hospital? What street? Where was your family living at the time and then move into growing up in Newark?

Bob   These things are hard to remember. It's been a long time, I wish my sister was here to help me remember these things because it would be more fuller. In terms of facts or what I can remember, I believe I was born in Beth Israel Hospital. It was the hospital that was on the hill sort of about a mile away more towards East Orange, and my family was living on 56 Court Street at the time, which is now where the Star Ledger building is. Our house was on the corner of Court and Washington and across the street there was the First Precinct, and I always thought that was how police stations looked. Now that's gone everything is gone and nothing is left there but the Star Ledger building, so that was at that time.

Yoland   What year?

Bob   Oh, this was in 1944, the war was just about to end; the Cold War period was just beginning. We had a laundry on the ground floor of this apartment building and we were living upstairs on the third floor. In the apartment building were Italians; this was an old white neighborhood and many of the people were moving out and the black and the Puerto Rican community was just beginning to move in. So when I was very young my memories are that Puerto Rican families were moving in and we were able to develop good friendships with some of the kids living there. I remember there was one family that was on the first floor and that's where I learned about beans and rice and chicken. And then also on that floor were the Van Deens; they are still our old family friends who we still keep in touch with and whom we grew up with. The Van Deen sisters, Blanche and Trudy, would hang out in the laundry all the time in their blue jeans, so blue jeans were around in the forties and fifties, rolled up about three inches, which's how they wore them. And my sisters would all work in the laundry. I was the youngest so I didn't have to work in the laundry too much until I was in high school and then I had to. But my sisters claimed that they worked all the time. And they claimed I didn't work as much.

Yoland Try to remember what a day was like, in the laundry, in a working week—six, seven days a week?

Bob Six.

Yoland Can you give me a picture of what it was like from the time you woke up in the morning to the end of the day?

Bob Well, not too much because my wake up was to go to school. So we were going to Coast Place, that was the name of the school, which was up the hill towards High Street, three blocks away, at that time I was in the second or third grade.

Well, a typical day in the laundry is where I might come down to the laundry, my mother is already there, probably my father as well, and once in a while customers walking in. There is probably people ironing on the ironing table; there are certain days of the week in which the press machines are on. If this is when I'm very young, rather than when I'm a little bit older, there are maybe four or five African-American women working on the presses. Later we didn't have that volume of work apparently, so they weren't there, so my family was running the pressing machines. I remember the clothes would come in, I mean wet, and then you'd have to throw them into the extractor machine to extract the water, clothes were being taken out of the extractor. In the midday, my sister or I would be folding clothes, folding socks. At one point the clothes and the sheets were then ironed and had a band around them and they were placed in a large pile. And I would take those and begin to sort them out on the table. Once, all the sorting was done according to the tickets and how much clothes were in each package, then you could take those piles of clothes and wrap them. So you would go to the brown wrapping paper, pull out the brown wrapping paper, and tear it to the size of the bundle you were wrapping. I remember I used to like to wrap the big ones first and save the little ones for later, and as you were wrapping the clothes sometimes a customer would come in. I think my earliest memory is that when I was too little to do any of this, I would watch these people coming into the laundry, look at them, and draw pictures of them on these little strips of paper, these weird looking potato head people. My sister collected them. I think she still has them. But everybody seemed to me to be strange and disheartened.

Yoland   What type of people came into the laundry?

Bob   Well this was in Newark at the time. I was five or six. This would have been 1950 or around there, and so the neighborhood was changing. As I said it had been an old white neighborhood, a lot of houses had mahogany on the walls. And this neighborhood group was moving out so there were only a few people left, or they were still there but they were not very active. And the African American community was above High Street but also moving into the area. Across the street was the Coleman Hotel which was apparently a major Jazz location so that traveling groups would stop there to play. But I remember across the street was the barber shop, the candy store and across Washington Street was the pizza parlor, with Italians who just came into the country. As far as I knew it wasn't a coherent community. It was on the fringe of downtown shopping, five blocks away was Bamberger's. Another three blocks away in the other direction was City Hall, so it was not yet quite an African-American community, and there were only a certain number of Puerto Rican families living in the neighborhood so it wasn't really a coherent community. It was a little bit of this and that and the other thing.

Yoland   Was it mostly working class people?

Bob   It was all working class people. There were some white families that never left the building, so I guess they didn't have to work. Or it seemed to us they didn't. There was a hotel on the street which catered to single bachelors not to families. Our wash consisted of police shirts from the first precinct and bachelors from the hotel and then a few scattered families here and there. I don't remember kids coming into the laundry very much, it was mostly men.

Yoland   Now your father had enough of a clientele to hire two African-American women to work for him.

Bob   He had maybe as many as five or six and I was very small at the time so I don't quite remember, but certainly more than two. This was when he was doing wholesale, so that means you're picking up wash from other places. You're bringing the clothes in, they might have already been washed, so that means you're extracting them and pressing them and folding them and then sending them back out, something of that nature. Wholesale business is of a larger volume, so when that wholesale business was no longer doing well enough that you could maintain employees, you had to let them go.

Yoland   Why did your father start a laundry?

Bob   He didn't start a laundry, the laundry from what I heard
        when I grew up was owned by my great-grandfather.
        He came to Newark from China much earlier and set
        up the business so that when he left to go back to Hong
        Kong, he was old and probably wanted to retire, then
        he gave the business to my father. My father was prob-
        ably working in the laundry I don't know how many
        years before that occurred,

Yoland Where was your grandfather's laundry located?

Bob   Same place. When he inherits the laundry, that's what
        he inherits. All the press machines are there, the boiler
        is in the ground, I think there was a time when a new
        boiler was installed, which means they have to dig up
        the side walk and put a large boiler down there. And I
        believe, yes, I remember, we had this long stick about
        nine or ten feet long and we would drop it down there
        to see how much oil or fuel was down in the tank, and
        I remember my sister saying something about how my
        father seemed very proud that he had a business in
        which there was this large equipment being installed.

Yoland When did your great-grandfather come to Newark?

Bob   I don't know. From what we understood my great-
        grandfather came from China to Newark and was in
        Newark Chinatown playing mahjong or something like
        that and he died of a heart attack at that gambling table,
        so he was quite young.

Yoland So your grandfather was running the laundry after your
        great-grandfather died?

Bob   Right, it was his laundry, and my father worked with
        him and when he returned to China, my father inherited
        the laundry.

Yoland Did your father work in any other businesses or for
        anyone else before?

Bob   I heard that he once had a job as a waiter in various restaurants, and I think his friends had jobs driving people from Newark airport to Newark Chinatown, because gambling was legal then and so people would fly into Newark airport so some of his friends made a living doing that, but that was before I was born. I know at one point he invested in a restaurant in the country, around Budd Lake, which at that time was the countryside. It didn't last more than a year, so all that investment was lost.

Yoland   Do you recall any stories about how your great-grandfather got to the U.S. and how he started the laundry? Was he the only owner? Did he have a partnership?

Bob   No, I remember that in our house there was location where we had this dresser or bureau display with glass over it and all the family pictures were in there and we would go up to them and we would see that this was my mother's grandfather, or this was my great-grandfather, but those kinds of stories I never heard. We would talk mostly of my mother's family history. I believe my father came here when he was thirteen years old. My mother was living in California, in Bakersfield, where her parents did very well so her father would often go on trips to China. She went on two trips with him and on one of those trips he took some of her brothers and sisters. I think she was the eldest and she may have had eight or nine brothers and sisters. Whenever he took the family, they stayed in a protected building. Since he was wealthy, his children had to be protected so that they would not be kidnapped. On another trip to China, my mother was betrothed or arranged in marriage to my father. I remember she said she saw him through the schoolyard fence.

Yoland   Your father went back to China to get a wife and that's how he met your mother.

Bob   Yes, he came to the U.S. at thirteen. That means he must have gone back later because he married when he was about eighteen and my mother was sixteen.

Yoland   In Newark, you lived outside but on the fringe of Newark Chinatown. What was the relationship that your father had with the community there? Was he a member of the CCBA? What was his business and social community interaction?

Bob   I know that we all had to go to the Eng Association Banquet every year, which in my memory was always held in New York. In Chinese community, you have to pay respects to various levels of the community, whether you are of their generation or the next. If that generation is older than you or younger than you, there is a different way in which you pay respect. And there are different names you call people who are older than you or younger than you, or have different relationships to you. So I know my mother and father had to do all those things but I don't think my father was involved in the CCBA or any other social organization.

(Although he carries the surname Lee, Bob is a member of the Eng Clan. Lee is his paper name, the name that was on the papers his family bought, generations earlier, to come to America. This was a normal custom for Chinese to leave China.)

My father had a lot of friends, who spoke very highly of him, but these were more like friendships, not business or community social relationships. These were just people who he enjoyed hanging out with I suppose.

My mother was the person who, every month, or maybe more often than that, would take us to the family weekend gathering. It was usually held at the Mon's family house. These were social visits for the purpose of showing respect but also getting to see each other, hearing the news, chatting with other family members. So my mother would take us there and once in another while we would go to Ipaw's house on Columbia Street and then you would meet various extended Eng family members. It was not that often that my father would accompany us on those kind of trips. *(Ipaw was the Bean Sprout Lady.)*

Yoland   Were the Mons connected with your great-grandfather? Did they help him finance the laundry?

Bob   I don't know if Mr. Mon was connected to it but, I would imagine they are because later, much later, when I went back to visit Toisan and visited the particular farming village that our family came from, which was Cai Mar Sar, it was pointed out to me that Mr. Mon's house or the Mon family house was here. And our house was there and so basically we came from the same village, so that we are basically Leungs or Engs. Mr. Mon was educated. He had a college education; he was a deacon in Old First Church, the major church in Newark, right on Broad Street. So, he was seen by many people in Newark Chinatown community as a kind of leader. And when people went to his house to visit, he would help them do various things, like trying to get legal papers or trying to write a letter to somebody.

Yoland   Did any other Chinese from Newark Chinatown visit the store or socialize in the laundry at any time?

Bob   In terms of Chinese people, I don't remember exactly anybody hanging out. My mother would be taking care of the laundry, my father would be off with his friends, and it wasn't too often that he would bring them back to the laundry. There was a laundry up Washington Street about five blocks away, near the A &P. In Chinatown there was another small hand laundry. There was an old guy in there, his hair was white, big bushy white hair, and I remember him as being sort of stooped over and once in a while he would come to our laundry to sit and talk. What I understood about him was that he was part of the bachelor society. He was never able to get his wife here so he had lived most of his life as a lonely bachelor. I remember seeing him walk away, sort of stooped over, back to his laundry. I remember now my father's brother, Sooki, who on occasion would stop by the laundry go upstairs to our apartment on the third floor, but he never stayed in the laundry.

(The bachelor society refers to the men who came to the US and could not bring their wives and so lived as bachelors for their entire life, they lived as lonely men. There were many Chinese men in this situation.)

Yoland   When you were going through Newark Chinatown at that time, do you recall any other laundries other than the ones you mentioned?

Bob   Oh there were laundries all over the place. I mean, that's what everybody did and lots of our relatives had laundries in the African-American community in and above High Street and in other parts of Newark. Laundries were a big thing, hand laundries where you could get your clothes done and finished by hand, and I think in New York, there was the Laundryman's Association.

Yoland   Was your father a member of this organization?

Bob   I imagine he had friends who were a part of it and he might have been a member but I don't think so. He wasn't the type of person who'd become a member of something. He had friends whom he hung out with and they did things together.

21- Victoria Eng in front of Chin Laundry next to Mulberry Arcade 1940's, courtesy Frank Eng.

PART 4

THE OLD TIME LAUNDRY BUSINESS

22- Murphy Varnish Company 1800s, a source of pollution and contamination in early Newark, building still exists, courtesy NJ Historical Society.

I

NEWARK, THE INDUSTRIAL CITY

In order to understand as fully as possible the situation the Chinese came into, in Belleville and then in Newark, it is necessary to have an understanding of the psychological dynamics of the U.S. urban population at the time and the generation calling themselves Americans. Newark was settled in 1666. By the 1870s it had experienced the Revolutionary War, the Civil War, and the War of 1812. During the 1870s, the fifth generation of immigrant families who first settled Newark, were either still living there or had moved to suburbs like Montclair. Some had moved to other states. The families still bearing the surnames of their ancestors were no longer immigrant families; instead, two hundred years later; they were now surrounded by a new immigrant population. These generations of Baldwins, Cranes, and Seymours, until this time, had felt that these areas their families had settled were theirs. Up until that time, the mentality of the times had reflected the mentality of these owners of the land and the government they created. By the 1870s however, the great Industrial Era boom was in full swing all over the world. Newark was a hub of inventions, construction, and manufacturing on every level. This was a very exciting place and time for those who had jobs and money, and there were lots of jobs for the able bodied and skilled. The need for workers fueled immigration to Newark, of many ethnic groups here in the United States. The Germans had already arrived and settled in, but now came the Irish, the Italians, the Slavs. All poured into this major industrial city of the United States. There were no immigration laws, no quotas. The Civil War had been over for five years.

The newly arriving immigrant groups of first Irish, 1820-1840, and then Italians 1850-1870, fleeing famine and poverty, were seen as a lowly class. Industrialization had been around long enough so that the rise of the city with all its horrors was an acceptable fact. The women, whose ancestors had arrived here in 1666 as hard-working members of farming families, had now reached a position of "mistress of the house," taking care of house and hearth, as the men went to perform their business. The generations of offspring of the early settlers had now become the upper and middle classes of cities like Newark, Montclair, and Somerville and further west.

Physically, Newark and Belleville were like all industrial cities: gloomy, dirty, poverty and crime ridden. Newark was more so because of its proximity to New York City and, by this time, its easy travel access. The black soot of the city covered streets, homes, and people. The air was filled with this gloomy smoke from the coal used for heat and for steam to fuel factory machines. The dust from this coal and other materials settled everywhere and accumulated in people's lungs. The major cause of death at this time was from diseases like tuberculosis, typhoid, typhus, measles, diphtheria, scarlet fever, and whooping cough. The poor standard of living, malnutrition, and toxicity from working conditions caused large-scale breakdown of the immune system, making people susceptible to these diseases. Metal poisoning from the factories and mad hatter's disease, a mental condition, caused by the use of mercury in hat factories were all contributors to the death toll. It was not until 1915 with the creation of Public Health Services that investigations began into the causes of disease from the polluted environment and use of chemicals in the work place.

The Victorian Era ushered in a time for the concern about health and compulsiveness toward cleanliness. Foul odors and dirty clothes became associated with poverty, immigrant masses, disease, and lax moral standards. At the same time, increasing urbanization and industrialization in cities created more filth.

The cities were teeming with immigrant workers who would work for any price. Laundries were a necessity and factory workers working long hours, as well as middle and upper class housewives, could afford to have their clothes washed. This was where the Chinese came in.

In an extreme effort to distinguish themselves from these Dickensian characters, the rising middle and upper classes became enamored of clean appearances, clean houses, and clean hospitals. Cleanliness became a sign of one's mental and moral place in the society. Middle and upper-class women, because of their social role at hearth and home, were the ones responsible for cleanliness. Lower-class women, usually factory workers or domestics, also took part in this drive to change sanitary conditions, especially when their class was blamed for the filth and spread of disease. They were the first ones to do the wash, whether they took it home or did it in the homes of the middle class or rich. Soon they were opening laundries. In the *Holbrook's Newark City and Business Directory of 1875, published by Holbrook Steam Press,* there were five laundries listed. None were Chinese. Of the five names listed, three were women's names. For example, there was a Mrs. C. Phillipot who listed herself as a lace cleaner at 30 Cottage Street. Most of the laundries were listed in the immediate downtown area; however, none of them were on the main streets of Broad and Market.

This is not to say that there were not Chinese laundries in Newark at the time. As I mentioned earlier I discovered one Chinese laundry in Newark at this time located at Broad and Central Avenue that was run by a Sing, possibly a clan cousin or brother of Ah Sing, and definitely a member of the Eng clan. However, this laundry was not listed in the directory of the day and neither was the Chinese medicine store on Houston Street in the Ironbound. Since these stores existed in Newark, it is safe to assume that there was a small population of Chinese that frequented these businesses, and perhaps these were the very early settlers of Newark Chinatown.

At the turn of the century, Chinese hand laundries charged ten cents apiece for laundering shirts; two cents each for handkerchiefs; two cents each for cuffs and collars; and so on. Comparatively, these prices were not lower than those of other ethnic laundries. On page 110 of her article *The Chinese Of New York*, (p104-113) in *The Century: A Popular Quarterly 53, no. 1 (November 1896)*, Helen F. Clark documented:

> Of late years there has been a constant cry against "Chinese cheap labor." Whatever may have been the price put upon Chinese labor when the great railways of the west were built by these people, today it is evident to all who have studied the question that there is no such things as "Chinese cheap labor." Chinese laundries charge higher rates than domestic laundries. Chinese laundry men command higher prices than laundresses of other nationalities. A Chinaman earns ordinarily from eight to fifteen dollars a week and his board or lodging. The white or colored laundress makes from four to ten dollars a week, without board or lodging. The Chinaman works from eight o'clock in the morning until one or two o'clock at night. Sometimes he washes, sometimes he starches, sometimes he irons; but he is always at it, not tireless, but persevering in spite of his weariness and exhaustion. Other laborers clamor for a working-day of eight hours. The Chinaman patiently works seventeen, takes care of his relatives in China, looks after his own poor in America, and pays his bills as he goes.

All this changed with the invention of the washing machine for consumer use from 1911 to 1926. The invention of the launderette, with its coin operated machines changed things even further. By the 1960s the Chinese hand laundry was on its way out forever.

II

EXAMINING LIFE AT THE BELLEVILLE LAUNDRY

The laundry stood on a plot about 1 mile square in an area that had been called Belleville and is now known as North Arlington. Most of the land owned by James Hervey was undeveloped, but the area of the laundry consisted of two red brick three-story buildings. One was used for the dormitory and living spaces for the workers and the other was the laundry. In the summer of 1998, when I went in search of the laundry, I found only the tall chimney stack standing. It was attached to a low lying building whose base had been part of the original laundry. Inside the large room were varying sizes of pipes some of whose diameter could have held a standing human figure. The building had been converted from Hervey's laundry building to a large boiler room for heating the entire housing complex around it. The chimney had been re-pointed and probably rebuilt since the laundry days and it looked similar to the old chimney that stood there in 1870. The land which had been Hervey's estate was now filled with small two-story cottages built after the Second World War for returning veterans and their new families. The cottages had little gardens around each door and the first floor was ground level. As I walked around the grounds I spotted what had once been the dormitory building. It had been rebuilt into apartments. I recognized it from a picture I had found in the Belleville library with an interview of George Casebolt during 1930s just before he died. The front had been changed somewhat but the rear bricks gave away the connection to the past. The building now housed several apartments with smaller windows. The slope at the back of the building went straight down to the Hervey house and thence to the river. A thrill of excitement went through me as I walked the grounds, breathing in the air and trying to sense something of this interesting past, whose ghost had been washed from existence, and if it were not for the chimney, I would never had recognized the grounds. I walked back to my car knowing that at any moment someone may come out of their cottage and ask me what I was doing on private property. The day had almost turned into evening, so I knew I had to move on.

The descriptions of the laundry written in the time of its existence came from an article written in the *New York Herald* on February 19, 1871, six months after the arrival of the Chinese and during the celebration of the Chinese Lunar New Year.

> The garments are put into wooden cylinders that each contains four compartments lined with ribs, similar to those of a washboard. The rotary motion of these cylinders performs the washing. The cylinders weigh a ton and a half each. The drying is done by extractors, the size of a large washtub, but made of wire. These were whirled at great speed, with the centrifugal force driving the water out of the shirts. The sleeping quarters of the 100 girls and women working for Hervey are separate from the laundry, in a red brick building, which is well lighted and ventilated.

The men's dormitories consisted of a large room in which many beds were set up. Each bed held one man, and each man had a space in a large trunk at the end of his bed that was for his things alone. Some of the beds had night stands or little cupboards near them in which were toiletries and other necessities. There was no privacy, but there was great respect for one another and each other's things. Much later, when one of the men became involved with and married one of the Irish women who worked in the laundry, the group built them a private bedroom within the dorm. (*Newark Evening News,* Feb. 1872).

There are no records of women having been a part of the Belleville Laundry group that emigrated from California. Yet the National Archives transcripts of interrogations of Chinese traveling back and forth to China reveal that two children were born in the Belleville laundry and planned to travel to China with their uncle. The interrogations imply that these were children born to a Chinese man and woman who were occupants of the Chinese laundry. Here are segments of the interrogation. The information given here depicts life in the laundry and how the workers interacted with one another. It also shows that there were family members working in the laundry and that there was strong cultural support. The files deal with the children named Wah Kee and Wing Hop, both, according to the interrogation, were born in the Belleville Laundry.

Facts from the National Archives' transcripts of Wah Kee and Wing Hop, June 19, 1903

Date of Document: June 19, 1903
Name: Mon Jim
Date of birth: 1854
Location of birth: China
Date arrived in San Francisco, CA: 1874
Date arrived in Belleville, NJ: 1874
Time lived in Belleville, NJ: 12 years
Occupation in Belleville laundry: Ironer
- Wing Hop and Wah Kee are nephews to Mon Jim, sons of his older brother
- Wing Hop born in 1878: Belleville, NJ
- Wah Kee born in 1882: Belleville, NJ

Date returned back to China: 1885
Date of return from China to the U.S.: 1893

At the time of birth for the boys, their uncle Mon Jim lived in Belleville at the laundry. He was working there with his elder brother, the father of the boys. Mon Jim spoke about the day he first saw his nephew, Wah Kee, at three days old, when his brother brought the baby to him:

> My brother came into the dormitory where we slept early in the morning carrying a bundle of what looked like towels but as he drew closer I saw it was the same sheets we washed and ironed daily made into a lump which he cradled in his arms. He sat on the bed next to where I was lying and pushed the bundle into my face. I sat up and peered into the eyes of the beautiful baby boy, my nephew. I felt happy for me and for my brother. The baby moved its clenched fist slowly in the air and squirmed slightly, my brother smiled, I could see in his smile that he was happy and loved the baby very much *(from the National Archives' transcripts of Wah Kee and Wing Hop, June 19, 1903)*

There was a large reservoir in the small town with butchers and bakers. Mon Jim described the laundry as being on top of a hill, on a street that the Chinese called Laundry Street because it led to the laundry. According to Mon Jim, there were approximately fifty Chinese people in Belleville when he first arrived, ran by a man that went by the name of Casebolt. There was only one steam laundry there. They lived in a building next to the laundry with the other Chinese. His sister-in-

97

law was the only Chinese woman living with the men in the laundry at that time. After their stay in Belleville, when their indentureship was over, the family returned to China with the boys.

Mon Jim was questioned further about how many years had it been since he returned to China, in the document he states, "It has been around eighteen or nineteen years."

The Chinese were fired from the Belleville laundry in 1882. This means that they stayed working there for a period of twelve years. During this time, many left and started laundry businesses in other parts of Newark, New Jersey and New York. At the time of their dismissal there were sixty Chinese working in the laundry. Here is the story of the incident that led to the dismissal.

Six years after the Chinese arrived Hervey sold the laundry to George Casebolt. In a Belleville newspaper interview in the 1930's, Casebolt eliminated Hervey from the story altogether and claimed responsibility for bringing the Chinese to the Belleville Laundry. He alleged to have been the person who went to California and negotiated the deal to bring them to the town of Belleville. From my research and records of the day, Casebolt is not mentioned with the original plan to bring the Chinese to Belleville. It is therefore, my assumption that true to character Casebolt intended to upstage both Cummings and Hervey. The only mention of Casebolt is for the purchase of the laundry from Hervey in 1876. Some have suggested that there was another laundry and that Casebolt's laundry was different from Hervey's laundry. But this is not correct. I checked the records of Belleville and North Arlington and there were no other laundries of this size at this time.

After twenty years of running the laundry, Hervey decided to retire. This may have been his real reason for selling the business, although some say that his reason was that he had had enough of the Chinese. Remember Hervey started the laundry as a retirement business. He had retired from several years as a seaman. The laundry was supposed to be his entry into the gentry of New Jersey as he retired and lived the life of a gentleman entrepreneur. By 1876, Hervey was now many years into his retirement. It is quite possible that Hervey was getting on in years and did not have the energy to devote to the full time business that the laundry had become. It was also possible that as he got older he was having a difficult time finding superintendents who could work well with the workers. He was never satisfied with Casebolt, whom he knew did not like the Chinese. But he had hired him, nonetheless, because he was the lesser evil of the many men who applied for the job. The laundry had a large staff, and overseeing all the aspects of the business had become daunting, but it is my impression that he pretty much ran the ship. In essence, by 1876, Hervey was tired, so he sold the laundry to Casebolt.

Casebolt kept the Chinese working in the laundry from 1876 to 1882, for a period of five years. During these five years living conditions in the laundry deteriorated, Casebolt claims he had many problems with the Chinese. He hired a man by the name of George Cummings to do his job, that of managing the workers and production. Cummings also disliked the Chinese and was very stern, sometimes mean, creating a difficult working situation. The Chinese, who had emigrated from California in 1870 to work at the laundry, were all gone. There was now a new breed of young men most of whom felt that washing and ironing in the laundry was just another drudgery job. Casebolt had had several disagreements with Cummings about the amount of time spent on ironing the pieces. He was not interested in neatness; he wanted production stepped up. In order to iron the pieces faster the men would have to be less meticulous.

The incident that led to the firing of the Chinese was a very petty one in which a Chinese worker had ironed a piece of clothing with which his elder Chinese supervisor was not satisfied. The individual had been told to redo the ironing of the piece, whereupon he refused. When he was reprimanded, he went to Cummings, the manager of the laundry, and complained about his group supervisor's demands. Cummings then went to the supervisor and told him to allow the piece to go through. The Chinese supervisor unfortunately got into an argument about the quality of the work. He was then fired by Cummings for insubordination. The worker who made the first complaint was not expecting the situation to go this far.

The Chinese men in the laundry came together and asked Cummings to re-hire the man he fired. When Cummings refused, the angry Chinese stormed the laundry. By this time they had been pushed beyond their limit. It is highly unlikely this incident would have escalated to such an extent had the situation at the laundry been a healthy one.

The Newark Evening News reported that the men took up their knives and hatchets (used for chopping meat) and stormed the laundry. There is no actual report of details of abuse at the laundry, but it is obvious that this may have been part of a series of smaller situations that had occurred that were not to the liking of the Chinese workers. However, when the incident was written about in the local newspapers and in interviews with Casebolt, the Chinese were described as troublesome, smoking opium and gambling. All the stereotypical negative attributes were presented to the public.

Let us re-examine the migration of the Chinese from the laundry closely. In fall of 1870, Hervey brought 68 Chinese to his laundry and by 1875 there was an increase to 182 Chinese workers; one can only assume that the situation of working in the laundry was a profitable one for the Chinese. By 1882, six years after the sale to Casebolt, however, there were only 60 Chinese workers left in the laundry. The situation in the laundry had deteriorated enough that 122 workers had left. The Chinese left the laundry after Hervey sold it to Casebolt? Where were they going? Some were going into the various neighborhoods in Newark. Many had started the settlement in the Newark Mulberry Street area, and some had gone to New York City.

The 1875 census counted 23 Chinese in Essex County. Where did these Chinese come from and where did they live? Since there were 250 people in the laundry at this time, were those 23 in Essex County those who had made their money in the laundry and moved out to further their income, or were they newcomers from California or New York City?

During the years that the Chinese were at the laundry and after the laundry closed, many of the Chinese left and went into the city of Newark to start their own laundries, medicine shops and many enterprises.

Holbrook's Newark City Business Directory documents the following:

1880   Two Chinese laundries in Newark; one owned by Sing Gee located at 518 Broad Street and the other owned by Sing John located at 576 Broad Street.

1882   Nine laundries in Newark owned by Chinese. Most are on Broad Street or Market Street. Some others are on Mulberry Street and Commerce Street. This area is the new Chinatown.

1883   Twenty-two laundries in Newark owned by Chinese.

1885   Twenty-three Chinese laundries, including a laundry owned by Han Sing with six workers under him.

1885   A medicine factory on Houston Street in Newark run by Loo Lum Sing and Loo Chock Fan.

1887   Forty-seven hand laundries listed and one steam laundry owned by Chinese all in Newark.

Sometime around 1875, Han Sing, a clan cousin of Ah Sing, both members of the Eng clan, and the Chinese merchant who had assisted in the negotiating for the Chinese to be brought to Belleville left the laundry where he worked. He ventured out into the city of Newark and created his own laundry business on the corner of Central Avenue and Broad Street on the first floor.

The laundry is documented as belonging to Ah Sing, so it is possible that he had an economic stake in many of the businesses. Sing had six Chinese working for him, possibly men who had also left the laundry. The building is currently known as the Kislak building, with its brick shell covered in late-1960s aluminum siding. It is possible that Ah Sing did not stay in Newark but returned to San Francisco, leaving family members in charge.

Once the Chinese moved into the Mulberry Street area, the little Chinatown grew. During the years of the exclusion laws, Newark Chinese were very vocal in protesting laws and taxes passed against them and often would not participate in registering themselves as a protest against these laws. One such woman was Ma Shee Eng, who lived in Newark Chinatown until the 1960s. Over the years Newark Chinatown became a haven for Chinese men who were able to bring their families to the U.S. and wanted a life that was safer that New York Chinatown. With the help of Charlie King, they became partners in various businesses in the city. They were then deemed merchants and able to return to China whenever they wished bringing their wives and families back to the US. Newark Chinatown slowly became the suburb of New York City Chinatown during the nineteenth and early twentieth century.

III

THE CHINESE LAUNDRY

Life in the Belleville Laundry was probably much easier than life as a self-employed laundry-man in Newark. To open a hand laundry shop did not require substantial capital or skill. In the 1880s, it took about seventy-five to two hundred dollars. The biggest expense was a stove and the trough for washing. Partitions could be built for a drying room, and since most laundry owners slept in their laundries, a mattress could be rolled out onto a table or if one could afford it, a sleeping apartment usually could be had above the store. Hang out the sign and you're ready to begin.

Once they left the Belleville laundry and stepped out on their own, Chinese males turned to various organizations for assistance. A *tsu* or clan member may go to his *fong,* which was a group of people from the same clan or village who gathered together for mutual support. The *tung hung woy* was a village association that included people from different clans but from the same village. The *kung saw* or family association was for people of the same surname, and the *hui kuan* or district associations included people from the same district who spoke the same dialect. Chinese people chose the group with which they would be most closely associated according to their needs. The *hui kuan* tended to be a business association, and so its members usually were businessmen.

Starting a business could be an expensive venture if you had no resources, and most Chinese men who came here had none. First you needed a place, and then equipment and then supplies. If you wanted to start a laundry and needed a loan, you could choose which organization to solicit based on your connections to the persons in that organization. Of the Chinese who created Newark's Chinese hand laundry industry whether in Newark, or outside of Newark, many were from the same clan. In examining the records of Newark Chinatown laundries in 1883, I found that of the twenty-two laundries in Newark, five carried the clan name Sing, five carried the clan name Wah or Wha, three carried the name Kee, two carried the name Hing, possibly a poor pronunciation of Eng, and two names appeared to have no connection. In order to get the money to start the laundry, a person needed to find a clan association or business association that would lend the money, which would later be paid back with interest.

In the late 1800s, most hand laundry businesses were started with a little capital borrowed from a clan member and paid back in installments. To insure a clan member's role as an entrepreneur a small sum would be considered an investment. Thus the person would be considered an entrepreneur/partner and this allowed him to travel back and forth to China. To start a laundry, fewer than one hundred dollars was necessary to purchase a trough for washing the clothes, a drying room could be constructed, and all that would be needed would be the private area for sleeping. You had only to put out a sign and wait. The laundry man did the washing, ironing, and folding. Hand laundries of this sort were usually run by one person, although there may have been many investors. These laundries were usually housed in one room store fronts. If there were partners who also worked in the laundry, they usually slept and ate in the same area of the shop. The charge for shirts washed and ironed was ten cents apiece, lace handkerchiefs, cuffs and collars, two cents apiece. Laundries were good business until the invention of the consumer washing machine in 1904.

Clan connections did not work for all. One member of Newark Chinatown I interviewed said he had never received any help from any of these groups. He was an adopted child and I wondered if this had anything to do with his predicament. He explained that he was worth much since he was a male child, so his parents who were suffering from famine in China, sold him so the rest of the family could survive. He was adopted by a family who had no children in order to provide for the parents as they got older. His experience was that if you were not part of the clan, even though you were adopted, you got nothing. And being adopted, even though he was given the Eng name, did not create any good fortune and success for him. He lived in Newark Chinatown until its destruction and then moved to a senior citizen center in the area until he passed. Jack Mon, in whose house he had lived and who was of a younger generation, would visit him weekly to make sure he was not in need.

By the 1880s to '90s many Chinese who had come to America earlier had been successful and were now in a position to assist other clan members by giving them work, lending money to start up laundries and later restaurants.

Paul C.P. Siu, (Siu, Paul C.P. Edited by Tchen, John Kuo Wei. *The Chinese Laundryman, A Study of Social Isolation*. New York and London: NYU Press.

1987), in his research into Chinese laundries, found three types of ownerships: cousin partnership, non-cousin partnership, and single-man ownership. During my research I interviewed two families who remembered their parent's laundry in Newark Chinatown. Both had knowledge of the laundry being in the family prior to the end of the Exclusion laws. These laws prohibited Chinese men who were not merchants from bringing their wives and children to America. Other than economics, multi-ownership was done for immigration purposes.

The Exclusion Act of 1882 was the first legislation in the history of the United States that singled out a specific ethnic group to be excluded from immigrating to this country. The act suspended all Chinese laborers from immigration for ten years, and in 1892 it was extended for another ten years. In 1904 the time limit was made indefinite. It also stated that Chinese persons could not be given citizenship by any state Court or United States Supreme Court. Thousands of Chinese who were in transit at the time of the law's passing were detained and returned to China. The United States' Circuit Court further ruled that, because a Chinese wife had the same status as her husband, she also could not enter the country and those already in the country, could not become citizens. This was the beginning of the creation of what sociologists termed the "bachelor society,"

Human nature being what it is, many Chinese found a way around these political moves. A laborer is one who works with his hands. A merchant is one who owns a business and employs laborers. A merchant does not work in a laborer's position but in a supervisory capacity only. A merchant usually has large sums of money and availability to such. He trades in goods and keeps the American economy intact. Merchants, therefore, could bring their families to the United States. This included wives, offspring, and other family members. In my examination of the records of people who traveled back and forth to China after the Exclusion Act was passed, and those who brought family members to the United States, I found that many listed their occupation as simply "merchant."

This maneuver was done through joint ownerships in businesses such as laundries and restaurants. So for example, a small investment in a business, regardless of the amount, entitled a person to the title of merchant. Another tactic to gain the ability to go back and forth to China was to show that you had several persons indebted to you for large sums of money and that on your return you would be paid these sums. Somehow this entitled you to something other than laborer status. If you had enough money to lend out, then you were successful and had savings. It also ensured the immigration officials that on your return you could collect this money and would not be returning to poverty.

Laundry work, though fairly successful, was labor intensive, and because most of the Chinese laundry men in the late 1800s and later were prohibited from having their families here with them, their existence was a lonely and psychologically overwhelming experience. Outside of their own culture, relationships were usually very impersonal.

Customer's clothes were wrapped in brown paper for pickup, their name or number written on the brown paper in Chinese. Other than as a name or a number on that brown paper, very few non-Chinese had anything to do with the Chinese laundry man after they dropped off and picked up their clothes. Some of the customers were pleasant some were unpleasant and many were outright racist. It was reported to me that in Newark, young Italian youth from the Ironbound area loved to harass and rob the Chinese merchants on the other side of the railroad tracks.

A few people were friendly and became friends with the owner, but friendships did not include anything more than a cheerful exchange when dropping off their goods. Perhaps the lack of the laundryman's knowledge of English added to the frustration some may have felt toward Chinese immigrants. However, we must remember that the original settlers of this country were English speaking and resented the Germans and other non-English speaking immigrants, but no laws against their existence as immigrants ever existed.

Working hours usually started around 6 A.M. and lasted a painstaking 12 to 18 hours a day, depending on the volume of the business. All family members worked, even the children. The store was open for a half day on Saturdays, and Sundays were (the building now houses the N.J. Law Journal and has the date 1923 on top)the one day that his store was closed. There was no time for any form of recreation.

On Sundays, the Chinese laundryman had to buy supplies for the laundry and take care of his weekly needs. If he had time afterwards, he would visit some friends for an evening of *mah-jong* or *pai-gow* (pronounced "paijiu"). During the time of the Exclusion act, he was not allowed into places where whites would go for entertainment; he could not understand English so could not go to the early movie theatres.

But when would the Chinese laundryman have time to learn English? Speaking English was not a necessity. He never had any time to learn the language because his whole day was spent in the laundry and the only words he knew related to the transaction of his business with his white customers. His conversations were over the counter and quite minimal. All his goods were bought from merchants of his own race.

His incentive to become a part of the world outside of his laundry was foreshadowed by the racial situation of segregation and also by the fact that his drudgery took away all incentive. Since Sunday was his day off, it was a day for social functions for everyone. For this reason, Sunday in Newark Chinatown, or even New York Chinatown, was the busiest and still is the busiest day of the week. Restaurants made money from these visits as well. The laundryman took his family to see relatives, buy clothes, or to eat out. This situation still exists today. Today it isn't laundrymen but factory workers or white collar workers who are Chinese who gravitate to the Chinatowns to be among their own and buy their accustomed food and hear their accustomed languages. Many Chinese still work six or seven days a week, and if you go to any Chinatown on Sunday you can see for yourself that this lifestyle has not changed.

But from the 1800s to the 1960s, the Chinese laundryman's social circle consisted of the clan or village ties. This was his circle of community, regardless of what the relationships would have been before he arrived in the new country. He was bound to the clan. He went to the clan leader if he needed a wife, companionship, or, most importantly, money. Chinese laundry men did not become wealthy from their laundries. Instead they managed to keep all the employees of their businesses with food, clothing and some money to send back to China. In 1943, the Exclusion Laws were permanently revoked; Chinese men were needed to fight in World War II or work for the war effort. They were allowed citizenship and were finally allowed to freely have their families with them.

Chinese hand laundries in Newark, New Jersey, did not suffer the same kind of threats to their existence as in New York. New York laundries, started by Chinese, who had left Hervey's Belleville laundry, were so plentiful that in 1879 they were considered a menace by the white laundry owners. There were so many laundries and the competition was so fierce that laundry owners would not consider opening a laundry without a membership in such organizations as the Hip Sing, On Leong and the Chinese Benevolent Society. These organizations offered protection in Newark and New York City. They controlled where Chinese businesses could be located, and thus maintained good relationships between owners and clans through arbitration.

23-Gladys Chin and friends, circa 1950's, photo courtesy Sylvia Lee.

24-Chinatown Boys in front of the Canton Restaurant, circa 1950's courtesy Sylvia Lee.

LOOKING FOR CHINATOWN - 5

Gladys Chin

I met Gladys Eng Chin at the first Newark Chinatown Reunion, which we held at the New Jersey Historical Society in Newark. We didn't talk much then, but she called me later to offer her services as a travel agent in case I wanted to travel and we met in Chinatown for lunch. The friendship grew from that time on and we are still friends today, joking about being grandmothers taking care of our grandchildren. In my opinion Gladys seemed to be a unique member of her generation that grew up in Newark Chinatown. A very attractive young girl with a perfect fifties figure in her crinoline skirts posing at the Newark Post Office with her girlfriends, Gladys told me very frankly she and her girlfriends went outside of Chinatown to find boyfriends. She claimed there were no boys in Newark China-town so they went to New York Chinatown to hang out. Now I happened to know that Newark Chinatown had several teen boys during the fifties and sixties, but I understood Gladys comment when she added that all the Newark Chinatown boys were cousins anyway, the comment made sense. Although Gladys lived only a short time in Newark, she and her family spent a lot of time there. Gladys was not only precocious but she has a terrific memory and knew every inch and person in Newark Chinatown. Even now when we speak she remembers names and places as though it were yesterday.

A Remembrance by Gladys Eng Chin

I was born in Newark, New Jersey, at 202 Mulberry Street, to be exact. We lived on the first floor, or really the second floor. I lived there until I was five years old and then moved to 56 Green Street, just a block away and around the corner.

We had a three-room apartment facing the front and I remember I loved looking out the window and/or climbing the fire escape. I guess you could say I was a "tomboy." Of course I knew everyone in the building and would run amok visiting everyone, although most times uninvited. My favorite "hangout" was in the apartment of Frank, James, and Mabel Joyce Eng, who lived on the floor above us. Mabel, or Joyce as she preferred to be called, was like my big sister and Frank was my best friend. They seemed so worldly to me, since, although I had two older brothers and a cousin who were a part of my family, I grew up like an only child. All three went into the service when I was five or six.

It was a fun time growing up in the '40s...we were all so innocent and life was so simple except for World War II. I was the only girl in my age group who was "out on the streets." Fay Hong was a year older, Violet Kee Chi was a year younger, and later on May Young moved to New York City Chinatown.

My father owned a grocery store on Mulberry Street and I was always in and out and helping out too. I remember being the "cashier" on Sundays when people would come in to buy groceries. I didn't always make the right change, but everyone was honest back then. Work was always fun when one didn't have to do it. I didn't have to do it, but wanted to. I learned a lot being in my father's store. I even went to the "live" chicken market to buy chickens; it was always a "pullet" or a "spring" chicken.

I stopped going to the chicken market because of the "nightmarish" occurrence that I experienced. It was the usual pullet order and I was waiting for the man to clean the chicken, weighing about three pounds, which I would carry all the way home, about one mile. (Remember, I was only about seven or eight when I did this.) Usually the butcher would chop off the chicken's head and drain the blood, but this one time the reflex action of the chicken caused it to jump out of the man's hands and it ran around the market, headless. I ran screaming from that place forever!

Living at the Green Street house, our back kitchen windows used to face the kitchen windows of Shanghai Restaurant. We used to look up and wave to the Eng Wong family members and staff as they worked in the restaurant. Shanghai Restaurant was another one of my favorite "hangouts." I use to go up and "snack" on whatever I could get my hands on! Boy, in those days the egg roll and wonton skins were made fresh each day, like a very thin crepe and I would roll one up with sugar and munch away. I was a spoiled brat! Nah, more precocious than bratty! But, I used to pay my way...I would help the waiters clean and wipe down the silverware, helped make the wontons and package the noodles. I was everywhere. All this before I turned ten.

In those days Newark had a thriving Chinatown. There were several grocery stores and several restaurants. Of course the main commodity was the gambling. Men came over in droves from New York City until the police shut it all down.

In 1948 I moved to Kearny, New Jersey, and my father decided to go into the laundry business there. It was very hard for me to move from my old neighborhood and my old school, Lafayette St. School. I was in the fourth grade and hated to leave my favorite teacher, so I commuted from Kearny to Newark every morning to finish up my fourth grade year. Finally, in fifth grade, I reluctantly transferred to the Kearny school system but came down to Newark Chinatown almost every day and always on weekends. I hated leaving my old friends. I even enrolled in Chinese School just so I would have an excuse to go to Newark every day. I did learn a little there.

As I got older and met Sarah and Tom Mon in my teenage years, I became a fixture in New York Chinatown. I met Sarah through her sister Mabel who married my cousin, Joe Eng. I told them "they started it all." So because of that union, I was instrumental in having the "New York" girls meet the "New Jersey" guys, and several marriages came about because of that marriage. I, in turn, married a New York boy, since all the New Jersey boys were my "cousins."

During those times we had some wild parties, wild for those times, but tame for modern day. The first big party we organized was held in the back of Canton Restaurant which was on Mulberry Street, and that was a blast. The other big party that comes to mind was the one held at Stevens Institute, which I believe was through the courtesy of Henry Mon, who was a student there at the time.

We use to congregate at Old First Church on Broad Street on Thursdays for sports and get-togethers. We would come back to Mulberry Street afterwards and hang out in the diner for snacks.

No one likes to live in the past, but I wouldn't mind going back for a visit. Those were fun times. Gladys (Eng) Chin – Flushing, NY (Gladys no longer lives in Flushing)

Growing up in Newark
Robert Lee 's Memories of Growing up at His Father's Laundry in Newark Chinatown

I first met Bob Lee when I went over to the Asian American Art Center with Willie Cole to deliver his work for an exhibition there. Bob looked at me and saw I was of mixed Chinese descent. He questioned me about my background and we spoke for a long time about the movements of Chinese throughout the Caribbean and the West. We saw each other several times during the hanging of the exhibition and also during the opening. He asked me about my work and invited me to be a part of an exhibition he was preparing on artists who were of mixed Asian heritage. After the opening, we didn't see each other again until the closing when the work had to be removed and we went out for dinner and the conversations continued. The exhibition had been a success with lots of press coverage so everyone was very happy.

A few years went by, but I kept cordial contact with Bob through events at the gallery. In the winter of 1993, I invited Bob to my New Year's Party. My husband and I had started an art gallery in what had been the Chinatown area of Newark in an old jewelry factory. Bob had never been to the gallery, and when he came in he was surprised, stating that he grew up walking by this building to get to school every day of his life. I questioned him further only to discover he had grown up in the Newark Chinatown I had only just became aware of and was starting to research. Because it was a party and I was the host we had to put aside my queries and we made an appointment to get together and talk. We got together several times but it wasn't until the following year that I actually arrived at his gallery with camera, all my recording and lighting equipment to make an actual interview with Bob. He was terrific, to the point, very introspective, analytical, and very much himself. Over the years my friendship with Bob has been like that of a brother, we have argued, fought, made up, and still get together over a meal to just hang out and chat. Bob is married to Eleanor Yung, a classical Chinese dancer and founder with Bob of "Basement," a radical arts organization they started with Jack Tchen and others in Chinatown, in the 60s. She is now an acupuncturist and tai chi instructor. Bob is still in the arts even though the economy has played havoc with both of us. He has a daughter, Onie, who at this writing is about to be married.

Bob   My father was a patriarch. He is pretty quiet and silent. You don't ask him personal questions. The mother is the one who is always talking to you about things like this, at least our mother was. But if you had questions about his behavior or what he's planning to do or things like this, you may have these questions but you don't ask them. When my father spoke, we were silent, and there was a certain awe in which when he said something, you paid the respect of listening to him; to what he had to say, and his words were very well chosen, when he did speak.

Yoland   Did your father send money back to China? Did he have any intention of returning to China?

Bob   What I know, and this is may be something that probably my mother told me or something I heard, I don't quite remember, but I am sure he sent money back to China. He sent money back to people my mother didn't approve of. I know he loaned money that he never got paid back and this was something that sort of happened. It wasn't a big deal apparently. Whether he wanted to go back to China, I never knew, whether he would even express this to anyone. But one of the things you do when you come to America is you send money back and you take care of a lot of people back in China.

Yoland   Now you went to Lafayette St. School in the neighborhood, and then you went to East Side High and you played with the children in the neighborhood. What was your relationship to your non-Chinese playmates? Your father owns a laundry so what was the class structure, what was the relationship you had in that class structure that existed in school and in the community?

Bob   Well, the first school I went to was Coast Place. It was about two to three blocks up the hill from my house not quite on High Street. It was a small school that only went up to the third grade. I only remember that when I graduated from there they awarded me with a book called Black Beauty , which I probably still have, about a horse, and from there I transferred to Lafayette Street School. The thing is, that it's sort of out of our district. I think that it's possible that the way I got into this school was, my mother probably said I lived at Mr. Mon's house which was within the district for Lafayette Street School. But I actually was pretty far away from that neighborhood, which was the Ironbound and an Italian and Portuguese neighborhood. So for us Chinese family we were not associated with that neighborhood. You had to pass through City Hall, you had to pass through Newark Chinatown, you had to cross over McCarter Highway and walk into the Ironbound section before you got there. After school I always had to come back to the laundry to work. So I never really integrated into the Chinese, Italian, or Portuguese community. And I wouldn't go back all the way over there to associate with the friends I had made. From where we lived the African-American community was really a couple blocks away, around High Street

116

and above High Street, and we weren't supposed
to go there. So I found myself playing with a certain group in my immediate area and we weren't
supposed to go too far out of that area. But walking through Chinatown as a small child was out
of the question. We couldn't go too far in either
direction, all these things were restricted. But I
had friends.

There were families in Newark Chinatown;
the few Chinese children who were my age when
I was growing up were maybe three. For some
reason my sister's generation probably had about
thirty, but my generation didn't have any kids.
We weren't hanging around with the Chinatown
generation they were older than us so there was
only a few in Chinatown that I hung out with.
And once in a while I was able to get together
with them and play. But when you talk about a
kind of participation in a kind of social context,
it didn't exist. This was a fragmented part of
Newark in which for me, the whole sense of time
was fragmented, a dislocated community. The
neighborhood was not a place that was together
in any way. And if you think of my family's participation on some level of social context that had
some kind of tie, some kind of structure, then of
course you do have the fact that we were part of
the Eng family that was basically living in the
city of Newark. Many years later one relative told
me the Engs came to two locations in the United
States, one is Newark and the other was Florida.
I've never been to this town in Florida, I don't
know where it is but this connection is certainly
my family. My family had a place in the family
connection in Newark and they knew all the people, who they were and how they were related to
us and they knew who was who in the village in
China, and these things carried over to the relationships that existed in the Newark Chinatown
community but these were things that were to-

tally alien and obscure to me and my sisters because we had never been to China. We behaved as we were told.

Yoland   Would you say that you grew up in a typical middle-class or working-class American way?

Bob   My father had a business so we had a certain security in that he was able to provide. Mr. Van Deen, the father of the white family who lived in our building, worked at times and during the Depression or at some point I know he had his own business and I know he felt proud that he was able to do that. So in other ways we were all just as far as I was concerned the same kind of working class so there was no looking up or looking down or whatever towards anyone. When the wholesale business was no longer viable and we didn't have a lot of employees, then it was just a family business and my mother had to work seven days a week till late hours. We, the children were working down there too, so there was no sense of class relationship. The only time I ever got a sense of that was later when I went to college. I went to Rutgers and I was with a lot of other American people, most of whom were Jewish, and I had a scholarship that paid the tuition. You know people at Rutgers were coming from a middle-class background then. They were living in the suburbs and other parts of New Jersey and in that sense I definitely felt a kind of difference.

Yoland   Who were some of your father's friends?

Bob   The one I knew of was Bucky. I knew him by the name Bucky. He was the father of Gladys. Gladys was a good friend of my sisters, she was their generation. Aside from Bucky, I'm not sure whom else I could mention. I could mention Segat, the husband of Norma Eng Wong, he ran the Shanghai restaurant on Mulberry Street, and I knew his children. I had a cousin, his name was Grant and he lived near the Newark library at that time and I think his family had a laundry there.

PART 5

THE MAKING OF CHINATOWN, NEWARK

U. S. DEPARTMENT OF LABOR
IMMIGRATION SERVICE

New York, N.Y.

April 3, 1931.

To................ Commissioner of Immigration,
Officer in Charge, Immigration Service,
.... Ellis Island, N.Y.N.,

Age 58; height
5'9"; occupation merchant;
scar left back neck; pit
left corner mouth; pit
over inner end of each
eyebrow.

SIR: It being my intention to leave the United St
porary visit abroad, departing and returning throug

port of entry of .... Seattle, Washington,...........
apply, under the provisions of Rule 16 of the Chines
for preinvestigation of my claimed status as an Am
submitting herewith such documentary proofs (if any
and agreeing to appear at such time and place as you i
and to produce then and there witnesses for oral exami
ing the claim made by me.

This application is submitted in triplicate with n
attached to each copy, as required by said rule.

Respectfully,

Signature in Chinese   簽 唐 字 名
Signature in English   簽 番 字 名   Chas King
Address   具家人之住址   c/o[?].R.Siasonello

相 簽 詢 委 亦 憑 國 九 而 來 人
三 名 問 員 親 擴 出 欸 回 亦 出
幅 裏 口 之 與 呈 世 之 茲 卽 埠 入
上 供 公 證 上 所 例 依 由 而 之
並 照 辦 人 查 有 在 三 該 去 港
附 例 房 到 驗 之 美 十 埠 將

25-Charles King application to return to China, circa 1931, courtesy of National Archives

I

CHARLIE KING, 1873 TO 1940'S

Charles King was a member of the Eng clan who was born on the second floor of 742 Commercial Street in San Francisco's Chinatown on February 9, 1873; three years after the Chinese arrived at the Belleville laundry. His father was the treasurer and bookkeeper of the store that rented the first floor of their building, the Hong Wick Jam Company. His early years were filled with the usual childhood things of that time, work, Chinese school, English school and some play with other children in the neighborhood. Most of the time, he would help his father in the store and other times he would help his mother in their three-room flat. Working with his father was special for Charlie, it taught him about money and figures and how they worked. Charles was tall and broad shouldered, with thick black hair, which he wore in a queue with a strong string tied at the end since it constantly threatened to unravel and embarrass him on the street or in school. Being tall made him respected and he liked that because most of the other children were children of shopkeepers or businessmen while his father was only a clerk.

Charles knew in his mind that he wanted to be a shop owner and not a clerk like his father, who was saving all his money to return to China. This meant that they could not live like the other workers who had cut their hair and adapted to the Western ways of living in apartments. The Hong Wick Jam Company, owned by a first cousin of his father, was a large company with many stores in different parts of San Francisco. The company had many connections to China from which the goods were exported, and to New York and other states to which the jams and other goods were imported.

Like most of the elders in San Francisco, Charlie's father had come to Gold Mountain as a young boy of fourteen, looking for gold. He had panned the hillsides and mined the ground and river beds for gold until that ended. He had sent for his wife and found work on the railroads for a while until he became ill with a weakened chest condition as a result of working in the mines. He was fortunate to have his cousin's store to provide some livelihood over the years. He was good with figures and his cousin had increased his earnings as the business grew and grew. He recognized the hard work of Charlie's father's budgeting and trusted and implemented his investment suggestions.

The years passed, Charlie's parents decided to return to China to live in the comfort they had worked hard to secure. They were now entering their sixties. Charlie was fifteen, and he decided to stay in America, continue to live in one room of the flat and rent out the other rooms. He took over his father's job, eating his meals in the store where his father sat day in and day out working on the accounts, but he disliked working with the figures in the dark room every day.

Sometimes he would go out and walk around the city and look and see what life was like for other people. He noticed how the wealthy men did nothing but sit around and talk, smoke cigars, visit their businesses, make decisions, and give orders to their supervisors who then passed the information to the workers who were the only ones who really did any handwork. He would return to the small dark office with its dusty soot filled windows and dank, musty smell of paper and stale food cooked on the small stove in the corner of the room. Since he had rented out two of the rooms in the apartment, he had kept his mother and father's bedroom as his own and in which he slept. There were so many people looking for rooms that he got a very good price for each room and his cousin had allowed him to do this liking that the young man had a very businesslike approach to his life.

Charles's cousin never assumed that Charles had no intention of making these ledgers, books, and abacuses his career. Charles knew this was not the life for him. He saw himself as an American, not a Chinese American or Chinese, but an American with all the rights to success that all other Americans were entitled. He wanted to break out of the mold. He wanted to get away from all the things he saw around him and free himself from the bondage of being Chinese in America. He wanted to be a person, to be seen as a person to be respected as a person. Charles was the new "Chinese American," but he was ahead of his time.

Charles had a goal but how to accomplish this was not a certainty. He was sixteen, ready for any adventure and excitement that would get him his future as he saw it, and San Francisco's Chinatown was too closed. A year after his parents left he wrote to his cousin Ng Jung in Kansas City, Missouri asking if he could come out there and work in his shop. His cousin owned the Hip Ok Jung store that sold groceries and Japanese art to the tourists of Kansas City. Newark Chinatown was also sixteen years old then too. There were shops, laundries, grocery stores, Chinese medicine shops, and gambling parlors, but it was disorganized and considered a dirty, dangerous place. Charles had only heard about it in passing.

Kansas City, as it became known by a decree in 1889, had grown from 500 residents to 60,000 in 1840, and adopted a new city charter. At the time of Charlie's arrival in Kansas City, the city was run by an Irish American politician named James Pendergast. In true Irish fashion Pendergast had collected his friends and his votes from helping those who were in need. In return he received their help in building his "monolithic system of patronage" to make Kansas City a mini-Tammany Hall. Because Kansas City was a small city in comparison to San Francisco, Charles was able to make friends and study the workings of the Pendergast method of city government. He became well known as a fair dealing but shrewd young business man and made his cousin's business more successful than it had been. Kansas City was known for its gambling parlors, dance halls, prostitution, and other forms of "vice." This was the draw to all the big spenders and traveling businessmen that moved across America at that time. The streets were still unpaved and the buildings looked more like a scene from a Warner Brothers cowboy mining town.

In 1893, the Geary Act extended the Chinese Exclusion Act for another ten years. For Charles and his cousin, born in San Francisco and already speaking English, this was not a problem, but for many who were hoping for the end of Exclusion, thinking of having their families with them or returning with the intention of going back and forth, this meant being stranded in the United States unless they could achieve merchant status. Charles decided to improve his English and attended a small private school run by one of the churches in the area. He wanted to get rid of the Chinese intonations; he wanted a smooth American style of speech. It was in this setting that Charles met and became involved with an American girl named Effie May. Effie was five-feet-four, with light brown almost blond curls and sweet smooth rosy cheeks that bunched up under her eyes when she smiled. She served food in the kitchen of the Christian Hall; sometimes she helped with the cooking. She was Scotch Irish and could be quiet as a mouse and yet fiery and raging as a forest fire, or so Charlie said. He loved her liveliness and her laughter. She taught him how to dance and they would often dance the night away at the town dances. Soon she was coming over to the shop to help with selling and stocking the shelves, then later she started cooking for the young men. The three of them often spent the weekends riding in the hills, singing at the Christian Hall and they taught her how to play pai gu, and Mahjong. They were young and they were happy. Charles had cut his hair and now wore only western clothes including a black bowler hat that all the politicians wore. He was going to be famous and wealthy and they all knew it.

But how was it possible for a young Chinese man to marry a Scotch-American woman? Charles waited and waited, not knowing how to bring up the question.

He knew there was talk about their relationship, but he and Effie had been very clear not to make it a shameful situation for her as a woman or a problem for him as an immigrant Chinese male. But then, it was Kansas City, and on a certain level no one really cared. It was difficult, but they worked with it and then circumstances created a change for Charles. In 1894, five years after his arrival, his cousin became very ill and died. Effie May started helping more and more in the shop. He would have to ask her to marry him. Charles had been writing often to a cousin who had left California to go to Newark to work in a laundry there. He told Charlie about a city that had much opportunity and no rules and laws that prohibited Chinese men from being prosperous. He invited Charles to come east. Charles decided to take the offer, and one Saturday morning as Effie arrived at his shop door to work, he grabbed her hand and pressed it to his lips. She was touched and smiled. "I want to marry you," he said. She had been waiting for a long time to hear this but knew that because of the difference in their races, Charles may not propose to her. Many times she had wondered if she should tell him she wanted to be with him so much that even if he did not marry her she wanted to be with him, but she dared not because of her religious beliefs and the fact that if she did so they would be looked down on in the eyes of the towns people who respected them both. She threw her arms about him and they hugged closer than they had allowed themselves to do so ever before. It took about a month to sell the shop and plan the wedding. It was held at the Christian Hall, and she wore a white gown, a very expensive white gown that Charles had specially made for her. She was his bride and he wanted only the best for his new wife. She became Effie May King, and two weeks later they took the train East to Newark, New Jersey. He was twenty-one. The Exclusion Laws of 1882 were in full swing.

It was in Newark that Charles's experience, working for his father in the shop and his cousin in Kansas City, would pay off in the biggest way. He knew that most of the goods in his father's store and in his cousin's store in Kansas City came from China or Japan. Americans loved things from places they considered the Orient. Since the Exclusion laws prohibited the travel back and forth of anyone who was not a merchant, Charles immediately on his arrival bought an interest in a small store named Quong Yee Hing, located at 24 Fair Street, which later became known as Lafayette Street. The store was between Broad Street and Mulberry Street, one block from City Hall, in what was already known then as Chinatown. He had used the money from his share of the sale of his cousin's store for the purchase. Most of the money he had sent back to the family of Ng Jung in China, but a portion of it had been his for his years of work.

Now he was a merchant and he began making the rounds as such. He could travel back to China and see his aged parents. Most importantly, he started making arrangements to ship merchandise from China to Newark via New York.

It was 1896, and James Seymour had just been elected Mayor of Newark. Newark Chinatown at this time was a disorganized enclave of small laundries, restaurants, and shops. The laundries catered to the workers at city hall behind which the community was situated. After work and for lunch, the city workers would come to Chinatown for quick cheap food, a bit of gambling and occasionally a drink. Charles saw Newark as a place in need of someone who was ambitious, calculating, aggressive, and ready to take the lead.

On his trips to China he brought back things that had sold well in Kansas City, such as jams, teapots, cutting knives for Chinese restaurants, silks, and gadgets to make the housewife's life easier. His store became known by the Victorian housewives for the interesting household gadgets he carried. The men came for tobacco and stayed to have a smoke and conversation; some moved into the back room to gamble a bit before going on their way. In Kansas City, his cousin had run a small gambling house for Chinese and a specific group of non-Chinese who participated in Chinese-run lotteries. Managing Quong Ye Hing Store brought Charles the money and presence in the community that he had seen others have in Kansas City. In the back of his store, he allowed the community members for a small fee to carry on their gambling activities and when the store was closed, he ran all-night gambling.

Fifteen years passed. During that time Charles who first lived in the Mulberry Street Chinatown bought out all his partners in the store becoming the wealthiest man and leader of the community. He bought parcels of land in and around Chinatown and in other areas of Essex County. He had bought a house in the suburbs for his family, because now Effie and he had children, sons to be sure. He opened other groceries including the well-known Wah Ying Grocery Store, restaurants on Broad Street and throughout Newark, allowing other men to be partners, giving them the title merchants which allowed them also to travel back and forth to China and bring back their families. He bought a stake in the Chinese Opera House in New York Chinatown, thus ensuring his connection to the politics there through his business and his love of culture. He loaned money at various interest rates to white and Chinese. He was now referred to as the Mayor of Chinatown by the white population of businessmen who ran the Newark area. This not only included Mayor James Seymour, but the Cranes and the Baldwins, who were also members of the New Jersey corporate business world of that time. He organized a group of San Francisco born elders and young Boston merchants to relocate to Newark thus ensuring their support of his political candidates adding economic clout to his position.

Charles assisted in bringing almost the entire Eng Clan to Newark, from their Toisan Village in China. Charles had learned a lot from Pendergast and the Irish politics of Kansas City. He took personal responsibility in the community, paid fines for men who were arrested for gambling and provided legal counsel for Chinese community members and merchants. He was an adept politician, and if he could have run for office, he would have. He made large donations to the various departments to ensure the safety of the Chinatown community. He was made a Special Deputy Sheriff in Essex County for twenty years, the highest political office any Chinese could hold at that time. As a matter of fact, no other Chinese or person of color had ever been inducted into the police force or government office prior to Charles until the riots of the sixties.

Charles did not live too long in Chinatown; he wanted the best for his two sons whom he sent back to China early on to be educated and raised in the Chinese culture. They returned as young men, ready to move into specific areas of their father's business, but Charles had other plans for them. He sent them to college; the elder, Roland King, was an aviator in the United States Navy and a graduate of the Massachusetts Institute of Technology. His other son, Raymond, graduated from Lafayette College in Pennsylvania and served as second Lieutenant in the United States Army.

I have been told that Charles took special interest in the young men of his clan and if he saw them on the street acting in a way he felt inappropriate or heard of any infraction they had committed, he personally would reprimand the young man and take him under his control. Frank Eng told me that Charles King had sent his great-grandfather, Eng Gim, back to China to get a bride because he felt that being single was causing him to act irresponsibly. Despite Charles's leadership, Chinatown remained a place of mystery and seduction to the outside world. The racism, the inability of Chinese males to find jobs in the "real" world, the exclusion of the Chinese from entering and participating in American society persisted.

II

FAIR STREET

The Gay Nineties were far from gay for many of the Chinese in Newark. When Charles King arrived in Newark in 1894, he knew that most of the Chinese who were there were from the Eng clan. He had clan relatives living there, and he knew that to be a big fish in a little pond was more advantageous for him than to get lost in the New York City Chinatown politics. He had written to the clan leaders in San Francisco and Newark, who later gave him a connection in New York City, so he was covered no matter where he decided to make his home base. But he chose Newark because he had a family member that had come over several years ago and worked in the Belleville laundry. This family connection was a member of the On Leong Tong and this tong would assist their own, especially an ambitious young man like Charles King. As a matter of fact, he was exactly what they were looking for.

Fair Street ran between Broad Street and Mulberry Street in the 1890s and was the early name for Lafayette Street. It was a major part of Chinatown in those days. The street was lined with buildings, many of which were originally homes built by and for Newark's small business owners, with stores on the first floor and living quarters for the store owner's family on the top two floors. By 1890, the original families who owned these had moved or had died, leaving the homes to another generation who broke up the one family brick dwellings into railroad apartments or rooms for rent. The first floors had laundries, flop houses or shops. These Victorian style red brick buildings and store fronts had a sour aging look. But unlike New York City with small tenement railroad style rooms, Newark's Victorian homes had high ceilings and lots of living space. Often several Chinese men lived in one room which would have beds wall to wall and they would share the kitchen in the main part of the house. The first floor of the building at number 18 Fair

Street was owned by Yee Yick and Company while 12 Fair Street was owned by Sun May Lee Company. These were two of the largest companies in Newark Chinatown, both involved in the trade of goods from China. They had the most employees and sponsored the most men to travel back and forth to China. They supplied businesses in Newark Chinatown, outside of the downtown Newark area, as well as businesses in New Brunswick, Kearny, and many other outlying areas. Chinese businesses went into areas where there would be no competition for this type of commercial enterprise.

Although the Exclusion laws prevented all but merchants and students from entering and leaving the country, there were a few laborers who were able to travel back and forth to China to visit relatives or to find a wife. These men were interrogated and had to prove their citizenship or their economic standing in the community where they lived in the United States or both. Visas for travel for these men were very costly so they had to prove they had substantial money invested in the community. Many claimed that they were the sons of Native born Chinese merchants who had returned to China, married, birthed them, and brought them back to the U.S. to work in their businesses after they had become adults. Newark had many of these kinds of families.

Customs interrogations were harsh, and many entering the U.S. for the first time used paper names. Paper names were the names of others who had already traveled and been living in the U.S. These papers were taken back to China either to be used by relatives or to be used by anyone who could afford to pay the price for them. Sometimes even relatives had to pay to get the papers of family members with which to travel. Traveling with these paper name documents required the memorization of enormous amounts of information about one's village and family members. Sometimes even the placement of trees and houses in the neighborhood in which one was supposed to have lived were part of the questioning and interrogation devices used. When a man wanted to return, he had to remember all the information he had stated in his first interrogation so that he could not make any mistakes since all the prior information was examined and matched to find discrepancies. Several men who lived on Fair Street were subjects of these kinds of interrogations. Chinese families were owners of small cheat books which they passed down or sold to others to use for entrance to the United States. Each book told the story of a specific family with a specific clan name, which was responsible for the arrival and survival of many Chinese in America.

26-Mulberry Street early 1900's, courtesy NJ Historical Society

27-Mulberry Street was always a bustling Market Street, circa early 20th cent., courtesy NJ Historical Society

28-James Seymour, Mayor 1896-1902, courtesy NJ Historical Society

III

JAMES SEYMOUR

Records indicate the properties known as The Mulberry Arcade, which was the focal point of Newark Chinatown between the 1910s and the 1930s, were purchased by Anna Seymour, the wife of James Seymour, specifically for the purpose of building a central point for the Chinese to live and have their businesses in Chinatown. It was also a commercial venture for the Seymours. This was the unrealized dream of James Seymour, who saw the economic value of it to the city and who also saw the complicated situation of existence of the Chinese in this country. James Seymour is buried in a cemetery in Newark, his grave overgrown with grass and weeds. His stone is a large six foot monument with decoration and his name, James Seymour, carved in the center. Close by, a slab of stone hidden in the ground, almost missed, is the only record of the life of Anna Seymour, his second wife and an extraordinary, dynamic woman.

James Seymour was born in 1837. He was an unusual young man with a flair for the adventurous. His father died of yellow fever in a New Orleans epidemic in 1839; the boy was then two years old. His mother remarried a Spanish gentleman, Jose Ventana, and they traveled to Spain to live. There James learned both French and Spanish and attended St. Austin's College in Cadiz. Seymour was a prankish child with a jovial humor about life. He must have been quite a handful, and at the age of seventeen he was sent to New York to live with his uncle, John B. Murray, a ship chandler who supplied all the outgoing ships in the New York Harbor with provisions. As James grew to be a young man working for his uncle, he found he could not fit into the prescribed path his family had intended for him. His uncle then recommended that he study law and put James to work in a law office; but this also did not satisfy the young man. James needed something physical and something that would tax his creative mind. He did not enjoy sitting behind a desk all day. With his uncle's help he landed a job working as an apprentice in the firm of Novelty Iron Works. James wanted no favors that would spare him the difficulties of rising from the bottom. He liked being around the "common man," and he wanted to earn his own fortune and not to be dependent on the favors of his well-to-do family. It was at this firm that James decided that this was a career that he enjoyed; he wanted to build things.

During his evenings, he studied engineering at the American Institute and became an excellent draftsman. James' career soared at the Novelty Iron Works, and it was here that he heard of a position in engineering with the Erie Railroad. He jumped at the chance to learn some other side of his trade and better his skills. While working with the Erie Railroad Co., a request came for the building of a railroad in Cuba, which would stretch from Matanzas to Puerto Principe. Although barely twenty-one, Seymour was recommended for the job.

The 1850s Cuba was economically prosperous despite the constant threats of slave uprisings, anti-Spain revolts, and the creation in New York City of a revolutionary group whose aim was to free Cuba from the hand of Spain, but to keep slavery intact. The United States had already made a request to purchase Cuba from Spain, but the request had been rejected. In 1852, the United States again made a second request, and that was also rejected. The United States government was beginning to realize it might have to wait for the Cubans themselves to revolt, but this could be problematic.

It was much more advantageous to either purchase the island outright, or to annex the island. The anti-slavery movement soon became the tool the Spanish government used to put an end to the revolts. Freed slaves would fight for Spain, since the revolutionaries wanted to keep slavery. On December 23, 1853, Spain made an attempt to prohibit slavery in Cuba. Slaves now became known as *emancipados.* The importation of slaves was punishable by fines or banishment from the island for two years. This did not, however, stop the importation of slaves. Slave ships landed on secluded parts of the island and carried on the trade. In 1854, President Franklin Pierce offered Spain $130 million for Cuba. When Spain refused a third time, Pierce made plans to forcibly annex Cuba by invasion.

James Seymour, now a young man, had heard about the fabulous developing island of Cuba and its adventures and opportunities for a young man with ambition. He left for Havana in 1858. In Cuba, James matured and saw a different life than the one he knew in the upper-classes of New York and New Jersey. The work in Cuba was difficult but not too difficult for a robust, determined young man. Malaria was everywhere, and the Chinese and Black workers working on the railroads were treated in ways James found difficult to reconcile in his mind.

On a return visit to New York, at a family social function, James met Amanda Elizabeth Crowell. The Crowells were a well to do family in New York and New Jersey circles. They were Presbyterian, and shared the same religious principles and social circles as James' family. James returned to Cuba, and after the railroads were completed he decided to stay on there. He liked the hot climate and the robustness of life among the Spaniards and mulattos. He wrote to Amanda often, hoping that she would marry him and come to live in Cuba. "Cuba is ripe with opportunities for success," he wrote. "We can buy a plantation and live well here." Cuba was a young industrializing country and the possibilities of sugar and other crop cultivation were endless. James was also in love with the sun and the slow quiet life. But Amanda loved the winter and the closeness to her family and she was not physically strong. A woman of small stature with dark hair and fair skin, Amanda Crowell was quite different from her sister Anna, who was robust and energetic. Amanda, first born, was soft spoken, retiring, and genteel in her mannerisms and bearing, probably taking after her mother. Anna, on the other hand, was like her father, bold and adventurous. Had James married Anna then, he would have certainly ended up in Cuba and the history of the Chinese in Newark would have been entirely different.

James returned to New Jersey, where he married Amanda Elizabeth Crowell in 1859. He had found the woman of his dreams, or so he thought. James returned to Cuba for the last time in 1860. He worked as an engineer on one of the largest sugar plantations, employing 400 African slaves and 250 Chinese contract workers, also known as "coolies," whose services were sold to the plantation for ten years. Amanda went with him, and while there she became pregnant, but the hot climate was not favorable for her fair, slight physical condition.

Although slavery had ended, Cuba continued to import slaves, but hundreds of thousands of "coolies" were brought in to replace or work beside the African slaves. James stated that many of the Chinese would commit suicide before their term was up and that on many occasions he would find them hanging by the neck to some tree limb or barrack beam with fruits or foods tied to their bodies, as they felt they might need them wherever they were going. James was obviously bothered by the cruel treatment of the Chinese and slaves at the hands of the overseers during their daily cutting of sugar cane, so he subversively began to teach them military tactics in the form of exercise, claiming they needed to strengthen themselves so they could work harder. Whether he saw this as some kind of means of self-defense against the political powers, and whether they understood that this could be used in this way, is unknown, but it does seem strange that a man working for the Spanish government as an engineer would teach slaves military maneuvers without some intent that it could be used. There is no record of what transpired in Cuba beyond that James tried to better the situation of the workers and was dismissed and shipped back to the U.S.

James made his fortune working in Cuba and returned home a wiser and richer man, but he never intended to return to Cuba or Spain ever again. Whatever transpired there that made him leave is unknown. Cuba presented for James the end of what he realized was his illusion with the romance of the Spanish culture and Spanish colonization. He had grown up with his step father in Spain and understood the culture well. He had, for a short time, secured a commission to raise troops for the Spanish Civil War, so his understanding of the slavery question was not minimal. Cuba brought him face to face with the evils of slavery and the, "so called, "contract labor" of Chinese.

After a year, James returned to New Jersey to set up his own business. He formed a partnership with two family friends of his youth and planned to open his offices in Newark, New Jersey. He had no doubt he would succeed. Newark was a booming town, while James was young, energetic and ambitious. The Crowell family loved James and he moved in and out of their lives as though he was a son instead of a son-in-law. In 1861, James and Amanda had a son, named James Murray Seymour. James Sr. was twenty-four years old at the time and decided to stay away from travels to be home to raise his family. His reputation as an excellent engineer allowed him to build a following in Newark, and soon he was planning to open his own firm. In 1864, everything was going very well when his wife Amanda died; he was twenty-eight. The Civil War was still going in 1864.

In 1865 James formed a partnership known as Seymour and Whitlock, which he ran until his death in 1905. In 1866, two years after Amanda's death, he married her sister Anna Seymour. They had their first child in 1870 and called her Amanda, after his first wife. The child, however, died after two months. He was elected to the Newark Aqueduct Board in 1884. In 1888, he became a United States Commissioner to Spain, and in 1891 he was State Supervisor of Prisons. James had a tremendous amount of energy and believed in participating in city and government regardless of his busy business schedule. It was at this time that he began to pursue a political career. I am sure that it was not only James's idea but also that of several of his supporters, for he had many, and that of his new wife. Seymour was well known as a man who believed in the rights of the common man. In 1893, he was elected as Alderman to the State Board of Education. From here it was a short jump to his nomination for mayor of the city of Newark, in 1894. Already the city government was known as a political machine, and anyone who went against it had a tough run. But Seymour had already built a reputation in the city. After losing the 1894 election, he was successfully elected Mayor in 1896, 1898, and 1900.

During my research, I found there was a lot of information about James Seymour because he had been Mayor of Newark, but on the other hand there was not a lot about him because he was a "friend of the common man," and in Newark that meant an enemy of the "the machine," as I discovered, since that was a name for city government back in Seymour's day, a term still used recently.

I imagined that James left his house every morning, saying goodbye to his wife, Anna, and took the trolley downtown to Newark. He would look out the window at the city as he traveled, noticing every person and every new change. The trolley traveled down Mulberry Street to Green Street, passing through the heart of Chinatown, turning at Green Street. It then travelled up to the site of the new City Hall that James had helped commission—a massive stone building with a large dome with stained glass on top—and where his son, James Junior, served as consulting engineer. James's ride allowed him to connect with the Chinese the same way he connected with them in Cuba. It allowed him to see the deplorable life style that the racism of America imposed on their lives. But, he was, here in Newark, as he was in Cuba, powerless to create the changes he wanted.

He had thought that being mayor could turn the city around. It wasn't until he became mayor that he realized how entrenched the bore of the machine had dug into the city he loved. So he tried to become governor. Maybe as governor he could do something to clean up the corruption around him. He lost that election and something in him changed after that. He remained the same James on the outside, but he realized he was aging and would not live long enough to be able to make the mark he wanted, to create the change in the lives of the working men and women of the city. So he would take the ride down to Chinatown, sit in a restaurant, walk along Mulberry Street and try to think of small things he could do to make a difference.

Seymour noticed the property on Mulberry Street between Green and Lafayette. He knew the Cranes and Baldwins had once owned this land. He decided that he would purchase enough property to build some houses for the Chinese, perhaps a little village complex, with a garden so the old men could sit and talk. He went home that night and told his wife Anna about it. Plans progressed, and several of his friends agreed to partner in the project.

Months later, it was April. The rain came down and a brisk wind, chilly and damp, stole down the opening of his coat, into his chest. He had not brought his scarf. The next trolley wasn't for quite a while. It was a Sunday and he had come down here to see what the area looked like without the usual weekday traffic. Perhaps he was returning from a meeting with the Chinese community members about building the arcade. He should have stopped at one of the homes of his Chinese friends and had a cup of tea, but he didn't want to bother anyone, so he started to walk. The walk from downtown Newark to Mount Pleasant Avenue was quite a walk on a rainy day. James had done it many times. He decided he would walk briskly and that would warm him up.

By the time he reached his destination. James was drenched. Anna immediately put him to bed with warm toddy and a pile of blankets, but during the night James developed a fever and pneumonia. Anna was stunned. This was not James, who never became ill, who had been drenched so many times, and who dove into cold sea water for a winter swim. She stayed by his bed side doctoring him as she was instructed. She remembered sitting by the bed of her sister and her mother and her father as she had done all her life. They had also been ill and she suddenly became afraid. Why did that memory suddenly come to her? Was it some premonition of James's death? Why had he gone to look at this property on this day, when he should had been at home with her and the family? He had missed the family dinner. Why hadn't he called to ask to be picked up? No, James had to be foolhardy as usual. She felt his brow and looked at his pale eyelids and worried.

In a few days, James began to recover from his illness. As soon as he could converse again he became excited about his new plans, but he suffered a stroke from the weakness of his condition and died. Anna, who had never really considered the possibility of James's death, never got over missing him tremendously. She had promised that she would continue his plans to build the housing apartments for the Chinese, and she did. He had wanted this since Fair Street had been changed to Lafayette Street, and the Chinese businesses and homes had been demolished. She had watched as the railroad bought up the property around Old First Church and the big railroad bridge crossed Mulberry at Hamilton Street. It took her years to acquire all the properties and find an affordable contractor. Anna was not a visionary, and with James gone and no one to run his business, funds were low. She kept her plans simple and inexpensive.

In 1910 Anna Seymour completed the building of what became known as the Mulberry Arcade, a two-story row of buildings running perpendicularly from Mulberry Street to Columbia Street in the center of the block between Lafayette and Green. The buildings, plain and without any redeeming decorative facets, had shops on the bottom and small apartments on the top floor. In the back of the row of buildings that did not run all the way to Columbia was a small garden. The paved brick street between the buildings sloped to a canal in the center, which insured that excess water would run off into Mulberry Street. After James's death, the family had thought Anna mad for continuing with this crazy dream of James'. Several of his friends who had planned to partner in the project dropped their support after his death. They could see no profit in this venture, and now James was not there to fire their imagination. As well, the family was having such a dreadful time with sharing James' belongings that Anna was glad she had control over the entire project. But she knew little of construction and so the project not only took several years, but ran into several economic and technical difficulties.

In 1910, with the family of Civil War author Stephen Crane, Anna finally completed the Mulberry Arcade, housing Chinese merchants and families.

LOOKING FOR CHINATOWN ~ 6

The Mystery Woman of the Mulberry Arcade

It was the summer of 2000 and Chinatown, New York, in the summer is the best place in the world. This was the summer I first met Leong Lon Youett in Tom Lee's butcher shop on a Wednesday afternoon, as I was on my way to a tai chi class at the Asian American Art Center. I was always several hours early, purposely, so I could hang out in Chinatown, talk to the people on the street and in the shops and visit Tom and Pam. Pam was in my class, so after my jaunts I would go to the butcher shop, chat with Tom and the old women who came in there regularly, then Pam and I would go to class together around 6:30. This particular day, as I sat on the big window sill inside the store, Leong Lon Youett came up the stairs carefully and entered. She was a tiny woman, slightly bent over with clear eyes and good spirit. As she came in she began to talk to Tom's mother, an older woman in her late seventies, she and Tom's father had lived in Newark Chinatown when they were young. They had had a store there, but later decided to move to New York. The women spoke in Toisanese, going back and forth singing the sounds in that way that old Toisanese do when they speak the old dialect of the village. His mother looked up at me and said, indicating the older woman, "She lived in Newark too." She then said something to Leong in Toisanese with the word Newark in the sentence. The woman looked at me and smiled. "You live in Newark," she said. "Yes," I said to her, "where do you live?" She pointed down Mulberry Street. "She is ninety-six years old,"

Tom's mother said to me. My head jerked back in shock as my face showed amazement. "She walks up six flights of stairs every day," Tom's mother continued. I looked at this woman. I was so amazed I could not believe what I was hearing. She was slender, not frail and shorter then Tom's mom. Her face was not too wrinkled, but with full cheeks and a pair of almost closed eyes she smiled up at me.

Immediately I wanted to pull out my tape recorder and ask a million questions, but I did not have it with me since I was on my way to tai chi class. "What is your name?" I asked. "Yettleong," she said or something that sounded like that; I couldn't make it out. Although she spoke English, her speech was so clouded with the accent that I had to listen fiercely to understand what she was saying. Among the many things I deciphered were the words, "I lived in Mulberry Arcade." I was again in a state of amazement. "What years were you there?" I asked; she shrugged her shoulders, then, squinting her eyes said, "Long, long ago, before you were born." She was a happy woman and not a bit shy, probably since this was her usual resting place before she went on to the next block and her six flights of stairs.

She and Tom's mom seemed like the best of friends. I knew I wanted to talk to this woman again but did not know how to press the issue. "Tom," I said, "can you ask her if she will let me interview her." Tom spoke to her in her language and his. They went back and forth. I got the idea he was telling her about the project. She looked at me with a kind of smile-laugh and her shoulders moved a little. "She said maybe some time," Tom stated. With that I was politely ignored as the two women chatted back and forth. The phone rang, and it was Pam asking me to come up and see her before we went to class. I said my goodbyes and went out the door, promising to come back to see her. It turned out that she came to the shop once a week at the same time on the same days. I went on to my tai chi class, but my mind would not leave the little bent over woman who climbed six flights of stairs once a week, to come out and get groceries.

I went back every week, hoping to catch the mystery woman of Mulberry Arcade. I didn't know who she was at the time, but having lived in the Mulberry Arcade was an amazing story that I wanted to get from her. I saw her several times again in the store and was only able to make a bit of small talk; she was always busy with her conversations with Tom's mom. A year went by and each time I saw her I made longer and longer conversation with her, telling her about my work on the Chinatown history. She knew about the restaurants and remembered the names, but not the people—but she did remember the raids. One day I met her in Columbus Park sitting by herself on the bench. Something told me this was the time. There was no one else around us on the benches. A group of old men sat at a table with black and white squares for playing chess, and shuffled mahjong tablets around, crying out from time to time and mumbling under their breaths to each other.

"How do you spell your name?" I asked and pulled out a pad and paper. "Would you mind if I taped our conversation?" I pulled out the small recorder and she looked at it and pushed it away, shaking her head no. I went back to my paper and pad. "Write your name," I asked, handing her the pad. She took it from me and wrote her name in Chinese. I felt a moment of apprehension; I had to ask someone how to say those Chinese words. "Tell me about your life in Newark," I said, "Why did you come to Newark? How old were you? Was this your paper name? Are you an Eng?" My sentences flew out of my mouth, then she stopped me and she said, "Too many questions, too many questions."

"Okay," I said. "Okay, okay," I said and nodded my head to indicate that I understood her.

She said, "I lived in Mulberry Arcade, don't remember number. My husband had a store in Mulberry Arcade; he sold things for the house, and some dry goods. But I was not happy there, so after my husband died I moved to New York."

"How did your husband die?"

"My husband was a bad man, he was shot, tongs."

I looked at her and my brow raised in surprise. "This was in the Mulberry Arcade." "Yes," she said. "He was a bad man. Paper husband, to help me come to America, paper husband brought me here. When my paper husband died, my real husband and I come to live in New York."

"Do you have any children?" She shook her head yes, then no. I could not understand which one she meant.

I was confused and amazed and shocked that I had found this woman. We talked some more about other things; she asked me questions about my Chinese heritage and why I was interested in this story of Newark Chinatown, and again I told her how I came to be doing the project. Many times I had to ask her to repeat herself.

We sat in silence for a few moments and then she said, "Time to go now," I thanked her profusely and she shrugged and shook her head from side to side with a smile on her face, mouth closed. I literally ran home, rushing past the fast New York walkers and down the escalator to the Path train just in time to hop on the train pulling out of the station for Newark. I breathed a sigh as I settled in the corner standing against the door and holding the overhead bar. I wanted desperately to find the newspaper article about the Mulberry Arcade. I knew I knew this woman. How is it that fate had led me to this woman? She was my Mulberry Arcade heroine.

Today it is 2011; I called Tom Lee today to ask about her. She could not possibly be alive now. He could not remember which woman I spoke about, so many of the old women had stopped in his shop to rest over the years. He said there was one who was 103 years old. I knew this could not be her. His mom had had several falls because she herself would not stop working in the store and was now in an elder home. I had a mental image of my Leon Lon Youett's form walking down the street slowly and wondered if she had had anyone there during her last days, if she had passed on. So many Chinatown women had traveled with paper names of people other than family. One woman I met had taken a paper name that stated her husband was her brother and had come to America that way. She told me that she could never live with him because she was always afraid that she would be found out, so they never had any children. I thought of all the illegals, men, women and children, still being brought into the U.S. in awful conditions, and I wondered if their lives really ever got better or worse or maybe stayed the same.

Miguel Santa Maria, an elderly Italian man from the Ironbound who remembered it well, told me the Mulberry Arcade was a housewife's dream. "You could get any household item or gadget you wanted there." he said.

PART 6

TAKING CARE OF BUSINESS

29-Mulberry Arcade Murder investigation 1924, courtesy Newark Public Library.

ARRESTED IN TONG MURDER HERE

Chin Fhiu, On Leong Tong member and Mulberry arcade store keeper, was impassive at police headquarters today while he was questioned about the murder of his cousin, Chin Chow, Hip Sing Tong man.

30-March 27, 1924, Chin Fhiu, who was found carrying the body of Chin Chow across Mulberry Arcade and was later released, courtesy Newark Public Library

I

THE MURDER IN THE MULBERRY ARCADE

The arcade lasted forty-eight years—compared to some of the other buildings around it, that wasn't very long. What killed the Mulberry Arcade? Was it the raids, the gambling, the "opium," or the illegal aliens? Was it the death of Anna Seymour? After her death those who inherited her properties allowed them to deteriorate, then simply sold off the Arcade without a thought to the people it was built for.

Within a year after the Mulberry Arcade was completed, the buildings were filled with shops. Most of the shops that had been on Lafayette Street between Broad and Mulberry were now in the Arcade. On a warm sunny day, Chinese lanterns hung outside the shops in their bright gay colors and red and yellow dragon streamers waved in the breeze. By ten o'clock in the morning the arcade was filled with housewives and very young children, pointing to the windows with their China dolls and windup toys and tops. Housewives handled the goods lying in the stalls outside or stood inside the shops examining the china cups and cooking utensils. Wooden stirring spoons with intricately carved handles, teacups and saucers with wonderful pagoda designs in that China blue color were a favorite collector's item.

Popular were thick fur hats for when the winter became very cold and scarves in bright colors and made of silk; and of course those funny Chinese slippers, black for the men and the fancy bright colored embroidered ones for the women and children. Every little girl had to have a pair of those in her Christmas stocking. In another store steps away with its awning opened to keep the sun from playing on the many herbs and dried flower petals was the Chinese herbalist. Here men from all walks of life came to purchase ginseng and bee's honey that would stimulate their sexual potency and housewives looked in wonder as Chinese women bought these strange looking herbs by the pound.

Business was good for ten years straight, and then things began to slack off. But by then the arcade had become a thriving business place by day and at night, in the back rooms of the shops or with the doors closed, folding tables were pulled out and Chinese men sat around in chairs playing games and talking in their fast sometimes loud dialect of Toisanese. With business doing well, it became easier to have sons and paper sons travel to the United States from China to help with the business. Legal help could be afforded to accomplish this and then there were the family associations and clan connections that gave one some security in staying alive in this hostile climate.

Newark was always the wild, wild, west, and back then it may have been even wilder. According to newspaper articles of the time, customers from Philadelphia, Chicago and New York, took the train to Newark to gamble in the Mulberry Arcade and in the gambling houses on Mulberry Street. No one living in and around Mulberry Street felt unsafe, but the media played up the area as a den of iniquity.

Now everyone knows that the city enforcement officials of New York got their take. The raids would be planned; storekeepers would be notified ahead of time and be prepared for the event. Each month the take was collected and all would run as smoothly as possible. The public would feel safe that the police were doing a good job to keep the crime of New York's Chinatown in check. Now every Chinatown has its seedy alley, where even Chinese people are not wont to travel at night. In New York it was Doyers Street, a curving, dark, narrow road that went from Bowery to Mott Street. In Newark, the enforcement crowd also got their take and there was a seedy alley called Liberty Alley. It traveled from Columbia Street to Liberty Street just at the right side of the Richardson Building. The problem began when the Newark law enforcement officials began to compete with New York enforcement about who was getting a bigger piece of the pie. According to Wally Soo Hoo, an ex-resident of Newark Chinatown who is now deceased, "Whenever Mayor La Guardia cracked down on gambling in New York, everyone flocked to Newark. Newark gambling became big stuff, and for a while there New York was a tight city. During Prohibition, it was hard enough to get 'tea that burns,' which was what they called "whisky" in New York Chinatown. But here in Newark, anything was possible.

In New York, to find a safe gambling spot, open all night, was impossible, so of course what did you do but take the tube to Newark, a very short ride and in no time you were at a table. If you had the right connections you could be in one of the biggest gambling joints on Mulberry Street, but sometimes the biggest games could be in the back rooms of the Mulberry Arcade. And then there were the restaurants. They stayed open all night just to serve the gamblers food. You could order a chicken dish or beef dish at midnight and have it delivered while you kept playing. At its height, after the closing in some of the Newark Chinatown restaurants, all the tables became gambling tables. The roaring twenties not only roared in Chicago, but they roared in Newark Chinatown as well.

According to Newark newspapers of the 1910s and 1920s, *tong* warfare was an everyday situation in Newark Chinatown.

Strangely enough, when I spoke to the Chinese elders about this, they claimed to have no knowledge of its existence except when they read about it in the newspaper the following day. One ninety-year-old man talked about the raids from the police but not about the *tong* fighting. It was all territorial and the feuding seemed to occur mostly outside of Newark, with Newark getting the spill over.

Imagine Newark as a suburb of New York. Most of the Italian mafia and mob fighting took place in the cities on the streets, very rarely in the suburbs where the big families lived. Maybe Newark was such a place, a place where all the big families lived. The Ironbound was certainly filled with its Italian mob at the time. I witnessed the remnant of it in the 1970s as the Italian families left for the Portuguese and Spanish to take over. Perhaps Newark Chinatown was the same way. Benny Eng lived here in Newark and was said to be the biggest godfather of them all, one of the most powerful men Chinese culture ever had in the United States. But let's get back to the new Arcade.

It is 1924, March 27 to be exact. A murder has been committed in the Mulberry Arcade. It is the eve of the end of the truce between the Hip Sing Tong and the On Leong Tong. The Hip Sing Tong ran all laundries and gambling joints (all in back of the laundries) between Raymond Boulevard and Market Street. The On Leong Tong ran everything from Market Street to Walnut Street. This included restaurants as well as laundries and grocery stores. The Hip Sing Tong had only laundries. The Hip Sing Association was a Chin clan organization. The On Leong Tong included many clan names and some of the trouble that caused the tong wars was the movement of disgruntled Chins from the Hip Sing Tong to the On Leong Tong. The On Leong Tong did not turn away other clan names but the Hip Sing Tong was a Chin clan-only tong. When Chins began leaving the Hip Sing Tong they became targets for death since changing Tongs was considered a betrayal of your brothers. Prior to the start of the On Leong Tong, the Hip Sing Tong ran everything; however, as other clan names became more powerful and wealthy, things changed. The formation of the On Leong Tong caused the break in the powerful struggle, and since On Leong allowed all clan names to be members, it became more powerful in all the eastern cities like Newark where the Engs and other clan names existed. There were many people in Newark who did not carry the clan name Eng but were members of the Eng clan. They had all bought papers in order to get to America, but were originally Engs.

So here we are and it is March 27, 1924, fourteen years after the arcade was built, and Leong Lon Youett enters the rear room of first floor of the shop at 7 Mulberry Arcade, with a man twice her age; he is forty and she is barely twenty. He is Chin Chow, a very important man in the Hip Sing Tong, and by American paper law he is her husband. He has brought her to America with papers that say he is her husband. In China her real husband is his brother, Chin Fhiu. If they were in China, all would acknowledge this, but here in America this was a secret, and she would be sent back to China if anyone knew. Chin Chow is a powerful Hip Sing leader. He has money and connections to get people from China to America. When his brother asked him to help get his wife from China he was only too glad to assist. Bringing women from China was not a problem for Chin Chow, especially since he could exact his payment from them once they were here.

He had usurped his brother's wife. This woman, the beautiful Leong Lon Youett, he had not seen since they were children. When he went back to China to fetch her, he was filled with lust and had no second thoughts about taking advantage of his brother's situation. Now she was his. Chin Fhiu in anger, had left the Hip Sing Tong and joined the On Leong Tong. What could he do? He was humiliated and quietly enraged. The American law could not help him.

For months the situation had been going on and Chin Fhiu could stand it no more. He had borrowed a revolver and invited Chin Chow to the back room gambling tables in his shop. Chin Chow was already very drunk when he arrived with Leong Lon Yuett and sat down with some other men there to gamble. He continued to drink till soon he stumbled to the bed and fell into the mattress.

Across the street in number one Mulberry Arcade, a group of Chin Fhiu's friends all members of the On Leong Tong, were sitting around, waiting, playing Mahjong. They had agreed to help and carefully planned this with him. The plan was very well formulated and, as with all plans, meant to go very smoothly. If it had not been for Patrolman Kirrane, all would have been easy.

The men who were gambling with Chin Chow stood up but stayed in the rear of the store. Leong Lon Yuett did not move but continued to look at Chin Fhiu, fear in her face. Chin Chow was a violent and aggressive man, she was afraid he would wake.

Chin Fhiu put on his coat and pushed Leong Lon Yuett out of the room and through the front of the store into the Arcade. She went straight to number one Mulberry Arcade, opened the door, nodded to the men and then left. The plan was for her to go to New York to stay with a cousin until all had blown over.

Chin Fhiu calmly paced the floor, looking at the game on the table, trying to concentrate to keep his mind on the deed at hand. Finally he turned out the lights; Chin Chow was sound asleep. The street lamp's glow reflected in the glass window of the store. Chin Fhiu's hand fingered the thirty-eight-caliber revolver in his pocket. He looked at his friends and they nodded to him. Chin Fhiu pulled out the revolver and emptied the contents into the sleeping body in the bed. Chin Chow never woke. After Chin Fhiu's first shot, the men joined him emptying their revolvers in the dead body as well.

By now the doorway was filled with the men who were playing Mahjong in all the locations in the arcade and each one pressed off a round of shots into the body of the dead man. The body moved as the shots hit it continuously. As soon as the deed was done, Chin Fhiu called to someone to help him clean up the scene. He had to dispose of the body, which was to be buried in the tunnel under the first apartment of the Mulberry Arcade.

About a half hour after the deed, Chin Fhiu with the help of his friends, was pulling the corpse wrapped in a blanket across the Arcade's cobble stone floor when Patrolman Kirrane, on his beat, saw the crowd of men and came over. He recognized Chin Fhiu, who looked up and saw his face; their eyes met. Chin Fhiu dropped the body and began to run towards number one Mulberry Arcade and was caught by Kirrane and arrested. All was over, but Chin Fhiu had saved his honor.

It happened on March 24, 1927, the day the truce ended between the On Leong and the Hip Sing Tong. Several murders had occurred across the country as part of the ending of this truce. Because of the number of bullets found in the body, Kirrane and the police department decided it was a *tong* war killing. Immediately after Kirrane called in the murder, the police raids on Chinatown began. The axes were swinging at arcade doors and at the doors of any establishment where any person was suspect or a possible problem. Men and women were hauled in. Any Chinese person caught at the train station or on the street was immediately arrested as being possibly involved in the crime.

The police arrested every Chinese that was found on the streets of downtown Newark. Leong Lon Youett was caught on the train station platform waiting for the train to New York and was brought back for questioning. Chin Fhiu was arrested and held. He claimed he had returned to his shop and found the dead man, his cousin, in the store and was removing the body so as not to bring bad luck to his business. No one had heard the twenty-seven shots fired, and no one had been seen leaving the store. The only problem that occurred was with Leong Lon Youett's testimony.

One newspaper article stated that Leong claimed that she was in the back room of the store with Chin Chow when the killer entered the room and shot Chin Chow. She said she tried to stop the man. She told the police that Chin Chow was her brother and she had tried to save him from being shot but couldn't. She said she did not see who had committed the crime since it had been dark in the room. In another newspaper report she claimed that the dead man was her brother-in-law. Charles King, still considered the mayor of Chinatown, the most powerful On Leong leader in Chinatown, came to the court to translate for the police, providing legal help for the prisoners. He asked that the prisoners be released on bail. The judge refused until all the investigations were completed.

Chin Fhiu was eventually released as a result of lack of evidence. Leong Lon Youett could not identify the killers from the line-up of Chinese men that had been collected off the streets and in the establishments that day. Shortly after the murder she and Chin Fhiu moved to New York City.

As Anna Seymour aged; there was no one to care what happened to the Mulberry Arcade. When she died in 1940, in her nineties, her heirs sold the property and from there on it went downhill until 1958, when the city condemned it as uninhabitable and tore it down. There were lots of stories about the underground tunnels and paraphernalia found by the demolition crew. When I visited the connecting buildings during my research I saw the doorways to the tunnels that had been closed up with cement blocks. Some led across and under the street while others led to buildings on either side of the arcade.(the building now houses the N.J. Law Journal and has the date 1923 on top)

31-Mulberry Arcade, circa 1940's, courtesy Newark Public Library

II

TONGS

Merriam Webster Dictionary
Main Entry: - Gang, function: noun, Etymology: Middle English, walking, journey, from Old English - *gagan*
Date: 15th century
1a (1): a set of articles: OUTFIT <a gang of oars> (2): a combination of similar implements or devices arranges for convenience to act together <a gang of saws> b:GROUP: as (1): a group of persons working together (2): a group of persons working to unlawful or antisocial ends; especially: a band of antisocial adolescents 2: a group of persons having informal and usually close social relations

The above is a definition found in the Merriam-Webster Dictionary as a definition of the word gang. Today in Chinese communities we refer to criminal activities as being committed by Chinese gangs. In the 20s and 30s, the word was also attached to criminal behavior in the Italian, Jewish, and Irish neighborhoods. The etymology of the word dates it back to 1632 during the times of Charles I. The first use of the word in a written novel appears in 1891, exactly the time of the greatest immigration to the U.S. The word most attributed to the Chinese "organized crime" was *tong*.

The 1920s and 1930s was a time of the first recorded immigrant gangs in the U.S. Chinatown was no different than the Little Italys or the Irish ghettos. The only difference was the racial difference, and that played a tremendous part in how these gangs were viewed by the press and the public and how these gangs were treated by the police and later the FBI. The relationship of these gangs to the community as a whole was interestingly no different than contemporary gang culture relationships in modern day Chinatown. Some of the names are the same, but the players have changed and the turf has enlarged, making the stakes higher. What is a gang, and what is a *tong*? In Chinese language, the word *tong* means "hall" or gathering place. How it changed to the concept we know it as, I have not been able to discover. A hall is a place where men gather, a group of men possibly in the same club or family or association. Some scholars say that *tongs* are American in origin; others say they are continuations of the secret societies that pervaded Chinese history and culture for centuries.

Secret Societies are recorded in existence in China back to very ancient time. The Chih Kung Tong, like many of the secret societies of the 1800's had as their major political goal, to overthrow the Qing dynasty (1644-1911) and restore the Ming emperor. In later years, the Chih Kung Tong relocated to Canada and the US and locations where there were large Chinese populations. Many other organizations, i.e. The Chinese Free Masons, joined this organization and worked together to establish financial support from overseas Chinese to aid the revolutionary army in China. Organizations (tongs) like this provided the desperately needed back bone for many of the struggles that provided financial aid to Chinese soldiers

In the 1920s and 1930s, two major *tongs* ruled Newark Chinatown and New York City Chinatown. They were the Hip Sing Tong and the On Leong Tong.

The Hip Sing Association was formed in 1855. Its headquarters was located in Manhattan's Chinatown. One time Newark resident Benny Eng (or Ong) was the Permanent Chief Advisor of the Hip Sing and was also the leader of the Chih Kung Tong. He had been arrested for assault, robbery, gambling, and drug offenses before his 1936 conviction for murder. In 1936 he was imprisoned for murder and in 1976, for bribery. He died in 1994 at the age of 87.

According to Bob Lee and other Chinatown men, Benny Eng was born in China, immigrated to Newark Chinatown and later lived in New York Chinatown. He was an Eng and was known by Bob and his family members as Uncle Seven.

The On Leong Merchant Association was formed in 1894, in Boston, by a Chih Kung Tong member. Ten years later, the On Leong headquarters moved to New York City, where it remains a powerful organization in the Chinese community. This organization ran Newark Chinatown for the entire life of the community.

On the other hand, the one organization that is not (knowingly) involved in illicit behavior is the organization known as CCBA, Chinese Consolidated Benevolent Association. For many years this organization was the mouthpiece of any Chinatown community, responsible for taking care of the elderly in the community, settling community disputes, and making sure community members received a culturally correct burial. It was the president of the Newark Chinatown CCBA who was responsible for sending home to China the bones of the Chinese so they could be buried in their ancestral grave site.

In my research, Harry Li Sooey, the elder, now deceased, was responsible for this, which leads us to believe he was, at one time, president of the On Leong Tong in Newark Chinatown.

Starting in about 1910, New York's Chinatown was periodically plagued with "*tong* wars." Each crisis was graver than the last, reflecting the breakdown of institutional authority and playing havoc with the lives of ordinary individuals. The normal conduct of business was repeatedly disrupted by outbreaks of violence, innocent bystanders were forced to take sides, and both the associations and the *tongs* increased their dues and extortion payments in order to finance their wars.

> The crisis was due not only to the shortcomings of the traditional structures but also to the exclusion of the Chinese and their isolation in urban enclaves. Many of the *tongs'* most lucrative operations—not only illegal immigration, but drugs, prostitution, and gambling—played on the desires of lonely and frustrated men seeking oblivion or lost in dreams of quick riches. The seemingly meaningless internecine "*tong* wars" thus have to be seen in the larger context of restrictions imposed on the Chinese. (*Chinatown,*
> *New York,* by Peter Kwong, p. 43)

> A major adjustment the Chinese had to make was geographical. When anti-Chinese sentiment deepened on the West Coast, the Chinese dispersed throughout the country, hoping to make themselves a less visible target, as well as to avoid competition with other Chinese in the narrow range of occupations available to them. In 1880, 83 percent of the Chinese resided on the Pacific Coast; by 1900 the figure had dropped to 66 percent; by 1920, to 55 percent. (*Chinatown, New York,* by Peter Kwong, p.38)

When questioned about *tong* relationships in Newark Chinatown, most had no direct or detailed information regarding its function. They apparently had either lived outside of specific knowledge or were afraid to give information which they felt might have repercussions. All persons interviewed agreed that without the *tongs*, it was impossible to have a business and that the *tongs* prevented their business from having competition which would cause them loss, as well as mediating affairs between community members or merchants. *Tong* members were very important community leaders and along with their relations within the Chinese community, played a very important part in relations with the outside world as well. The "Mayor of Chinatown" was usually a name the white community gave to the most influential Chinese person in the Chinese community. This person had to be one that spoke English and mixed well with the white community. He was well established as a prominent business man, moved easily between situations in either community, seeming to favor neither side, but ready to stick up for his countrymen if necessary; but at the same time ready to take the side of white lawmakers, should that be necessary as well. According to my research the first recorded Mayor of Chinatown was Charles King. There seems to be no mention of a mayor predating his arrival. The title was given by the white establishment, and this was always a person of means in contrast to the other Chinese in the community. He was sometimes president of the CCBA, definitely the president of the On Leong Tong. Where his economic wealth came from can be dubiously suggested, but regardless, this was the person considered to be the spokesperson for the community. There may possibly have been at least one other community leader before him; I have not as yet found any record of who that person may have been. Perhaps it was someone related to Ah Sing who sent the first Chinese to Belleville and who opened the first Chinese laundry on Central Avenue and Broad Street in the late 1800s.

How did *tongs*/secret society organizations get to Newark? When did they arrive and who brought them? They could have come from California, or, considering the proximity to New York City, we can assume that the connection was made with organizations there and may have come from this area. However, in examining the situation at Hervey's laundry, we have recorded situations of gambling, fights and community conflicts among the Chinese.

Were these just isolated incidents unrelated to any secret society connections and did they develop into *tong* connections after the workers left and moved into Newark?

The men of Newark Chinatown had close ties with New York Chinese community and moved back and forth freely in these social settings. If we examine the newspaper articles of Newark Chinatown carefully, we can note that the family associations, as it became in Chinatowns in the U.S., stretched to Chicago, Philadelphia, and to all the Chinatowns that existed. The associations we call the *tongs* were part of the re-creation of that familial support system that may have existed in the Chinese village from which these Chinese men came. "Tongs attracted those whose own district family associations were too weak to protect their members from virtual economic exclusion by the larger organizations." (*Chinatown, New York,* by Peter Kwong, p.42).

Wallace Soo Hoo states that his uncle started the On Leong Tong because he was brutalized by a group of Hip Sing men who wanted to rob him of his accomplishments. He was alone struggling to achieve some smattering of success. Wallace Soo Hoo came from Boston. The On Leong Tong was started in Boston. But were the roots of these types of societies an importation from China? The term *tong* seems to be an Americanization of what is similar in China and called a triad. The

Fuk Yee Hing triad society existed in Hong Kong before 1866.

By that time, many Chiu Chow people came down to Hong Kong to earn a living because life was very hard in their native villages. It usually took them a few days to walk to Hong Kong. On the way, the Chiu Chow people were often robbed by bandit gangs in the mountain areas in the Waichow district (the middle part of Guangdong province). Some clansmen found that the bandits would let them go if they were triad members. Thus, many Chiu Chow people joined triad societies for protection before coming to Hong Kong (HK Police Interview, 2 October 1993, *The Triads as Business,* Yiu Kong Chu, p. 19).

The power of the tongs grew with the profits from their illegal and underground activities, and they began to encroach on the territory of the regular associations. Conflicts resulted, but the tongs had a distinct advantage: their members were bound together by oaths of allegiance, they had a standing army of "hatchet men" and, being secret societies, no one was sure who their members were." (*Chinatown, New York,* by Peter Kwong, p.42).

I discussed the *tongs* with Wally and Frank Soo Hoo:

Wally: I never forget an incident with my father. Mei Tong is our uncle. At one time people voted every year for the president of the association. Mei tong wanted my father be a president, and I never forget that my mother said to him—"Why don't you take the job, it won't cost you a penny— if somebody wants that job they spend thousands and thousands of dollars before he can get his name to be elected—you know he helped you; he wanted you to be president." My father said, "Are you crazy, I'd rather be poor. I'd rather be starving," my father said to her.

"Don't you feel guilty, people come to the United States—some people sold their son or sell their house before they get the extra money to come to the United States—and you know many times they kill the wrong people. When they kill, they not only kill one, you know, they kill the whole family too."
My father said, "If they don't want me be their secretary or treasurer, I

rather resign, I don't want it."

Frank: He said this because when you're president of that organization, sometimes you have to give the order to go get that guy—get this person—but as secretary he was just recording the gambling money. He didn't want to be president.

Wally: And I overheard that and I never forget that. I overheard that at night time; my father and mother they talked about that—that was in Boston at that time. Every year, these associations, they have a fight over gambling territory, same as the mafia.

Frank: You overstep your boundary, you try to muscle into my territory, and we have a war. (end of interview)

> Given the severe limitations on the areas of economic activity open to them, the commercial expansion of any one tong or association automatically meant another's loss. Friction of this nature led to war" (*Chinatown, New York,* by Peter Kwong, p.43).

The worst year for raids against the Chinese community in Newark was 1927. There were over fifty-two raids that year, approximately one raid per week. There was also the murder in the Chinatown Arcade. This was a first of its kind in Newark Chinatown and created fear in not only the white community but also in the Chinese community who had up till now lived with the tongs without any major concerns. The murder was said to stem from a dispute over gambling profits. The murdered man was a member of the Hip Sing Tong, the accused a member of the On Leong Tong. According to my research, the Hip Sing Tong existed prior to the On Leong Tong and was run solely by members of the Chin family. They excluded other clans from joining the organization but afforded them protection. However, other clan members were extremely vulnerable to the ruthlessness of the Chins and did not have the privileges that Chins had in dealing with the organization. The On Leong Tong was started to put an end to this consolidation of power by one clan. The On Leong Tong allowed all clans to join the tong as long as they played by the rules. Chins who did not feel alignment to the Hip Sing Tong were not restricted from joining; as a matter of fact, they were welcomed into the On Leong Tong. Apparently Newark was On Leong Tong territory. Sometime prior to the 1920s, the Hip Sing Tong moved into Newark. The staked out their territory as west of Raymond Boulevard and opened some laundries in whose back rooms their gambling business proliferated. They were of no importance to the On Leong Tongs of Newark who owned everything from Raymond Boulevard east on Mulberry Street and many other businesses sprinkled in downtown Newark and the

WHEN NEWARK HAD A CHINATOWN

surrounding suburbs of the city. When the Hip Sing Tong realized that their businesses were not improving because of the proliferation of On Leong Tong control, they decided they needed to expand in Newark. Thus a part of the already ongoing war in many other cities between these two groups became played out in Newark streets. The murder in the Mulberry Arcade was a pivotal point in Newark in this national war against each other. According to one of my sources the murder provided the following:

1. Since the Newark Law Enforcement leaders were not getting a big enough cut of the take in comparable to New York Law Enforcement Leaders, this gave them a chance to vent their anger.
2. The murder provided a crucial context in the city's desire to rid itself of the Chinese and acquire properties that were slowly becoming extremely valuable in the downtown area.

Tong wars would continue for a period of years, then apparently the leaders of the CCBC or some other Chinese agency would be asked to intervene and they would stop for one to two years before beginning again. Previous to the 1927 *tong* war was the one that lasted from October 8, 1925 to March 25, 1925. Over seventy Chinese were killed in this period. In some ways I find similarities to the Chinese uprisings in China during the decay of the Manchu dynasty. On March 26, 1927, the *Newark Evening News* reported *tong* leaders as saying that there was no warfare between the factions but rather the nationwide murders and assaults were the result of "family and individual differences."

In the murder in the Mulberry Arcade, the murdered man had been riddled with twenty-seven bullets. According to newspaper reports, this occurred while he was in a bed asleep. He was a Hip Sing Tong. The accused was labeled as a cousin of the deceased and a member of the On Leong Tong. Both were members of the Chin family. Was this really a family feud? Had Chins moved from being Hip Sing to being On Leong members and was this causing a family rift? The case was dismissed June 30, 1927, several months later in a Newark court. Was it for lack of evidence or was the court paid off by the Association?

No one had seen the crime committed. There were apparently no actual witnesses to the event. The accused, who spoke only Chinese, was caught as he was dragging the body from his store with the help of some of his friends, none of whom could supply any information. The dismissal was based on the accused's lack of knowledge about the murder. In the newspaper article a patrolman was quoted as saying, "What's the use of running him in, they never can get anything on a Chinaman."

The 1927 *tong* war is reported in the paper to have been caused by the death and subsequent behavior of one Chin in Chicago's Chinatown. He apparently had become a member of the On Leong Tong, then dropped out of that organization and joined the Hip Sing Tong. He then reversed his decision and returned to the On Leong Tong, wherein the Hip Sing group accused him of being a spy. His death resulted in Tong wars in Brooklyn, Newark, Pittsburgh and elsewhere.

Was this really a clan feud that consisted of Chin family members against the On Leong Tong, or was it a turf war over gambling profits and territory?

The *tong* wars in Newark Chinatown, although frightening for the community of Newarkers living in the area, were much less traumatic than the events that occurred in New York Chinatown. In New York City, the population of gambling parlors and gamblers was much greater and therefore the amounts of money passing hands had to be much greater as well.

Even as the country's newly elected president, Franklin Delano Roosevelt, was taking historic economic measures to reverse the free fall into chaos and self-destruction, New York's Mayor La Guardia determined that the way to political and social salvation lay in moral redemption. After cleaning up what had become the most corrupt police department of any city in America, La Guardia set about to destroy the gambling sites and dens of sexual and alcoholic corruption that had flourished during the previous administration. With ax in hand, and newsreel cameras always close by, he went on a personal rampage against the city's amusement halls.

In the 1920s, New Jersey had the reputation as one of the most politically corrupt states in the nation. More than two dozen high-ranking public officials went to jail during a ten-year period, including a U.S. Senator, three Congressmen, two New Jersey Secretaries of State, and the Mayors of Newark and Jersey City.

III

ASSOCIATIONS AND GANG CULTURE

July 2, 2002
Interview with Frank and Wally Soo Hoo, brothers who lived in Newark China-
town. Wally is the older brother.

Yoland: Let's start with an introduction. Today is July 2, 2002. I am here with
         Frank and Wally Soo Hoo at Frank's house. Can you first begin with
         your name and when you were born?

Wally   My name is Wallace Soo Hoo Wei. I was born in China, in 1913. I came
         to the United States around twelve years old; first I was in Boston,
         Mass. Then I moved to Newark New Jersey, 1928.

Yoland   How old were you when you moved to Newark?

Wally   About fifteen or sixteen.

Yoland   What was the reason you moved to Newark?

Wally   It was the beginning of the Depression; my father's business in Boston
         was bankrupt. So we heard that Newark was a boom town, so that's
         why we moved to Newark.

Yoland   What kind of business did your father have in Boston?

Wally He had a restaurant. He was secretary and treasurer of an association in Boston, and he had a Chinese opera theatre in Boston.

Yoland What was the name of the association?

Wally The On Leong Association.

Yoland And do you remember the name of the opera theatre?

Wally The opera theatre didn't have a name because it was only a small theatre, 'round about 250 or 300 seats. The Chinatown people all knew that that was a theatre. It was right next to the telephone company building.

Yoland Frank, when were you born?

Frank I was born in 1939.

Yoland Were you born in China?

Frank No, I was the only one born in Newark. In that building, the Lun On building, on the third floor on top of the Sai Woo restaurant.

Yoland Wally, what happened when you came to Newark in 1928? Did you go to school?

Wally At that time I was in the seventh grade, and when we moved to Newark I went first to Chestnut Street School. Then I went to the Oliver St. School. It was a very bad time and I had to quit school to look for job.

Yoland Can you describe Chinatown to me, as much as you remember?

Wally Well, Chinatown was very, very busy. There were around 20 taxicabs in Chinatown to take people to go Penn Station to New York. Chinatown was very busy at that time.

Yoland Were these taxi cabs run by Chinese people?

Wally No American people.

Yoland So, American men owned taxis and they would drive people from New

York Penn Station to Mulberry Street.

Wally   I think at that time they charged fifty cents for each trip. If they went to New York through the Pulaski Skyway, which had just begun to run… it cost five dollars to go to New York.

Yoland   So what made Chinatown busy?

Wally   Mostly gambling. I remember they had about twenty different Chinese lotteries, and lot of gambling buildings. When I was there, Mulberry Street used to have only wooden houses; on Mulberry Street between Lafayette Street and Green Street, that one block was all old houses. Then the gambling started booming they must have made a lot of money, so they tore down the old houses and built regular brick buildings like 202 and 204 Mulberry Street, and I remember there were three new buildings, and upstairs were apartment houses.

Yoland   Do you know who built them? What organization or men built them?

Wally   I don't know; I think it was the gambling syndicate. I don't know who was head man then, but it was all incorporated, all incorporated.

Yoland   So those were built by the gambling syndicates. The people that were running the gambling built those apartment buildings.

Wally   They were all controlled by a company. The apartments and the gambling houses and the social clubs were all controlled by the same company.

Yoland   But they actually were responsible for building the building as well?

Wally   At that time I think the buildings and the gambling were all together and were controlled by the On Leong Association. The main branch was in New York.

Yoland   Does the name Lun On Company ring a bell?

Wally   That's the building, we lived in upstairs. That was a new gambling building. Downstairs was a restaurant. The second restaurant there was the Sai Woo restaurant.

Yoland   Who and what was Lun On?

Wally   Lun On was a company name. Lun On.

Yoland   Was it connected to the On Leong?

Wally   Oh yes.

Yoland   Who were some of the people who ran this organization—could you give me some of the names of the people who were in charge of that?

Wally   The On Leong Association have every year a new president; they vote every year for a new chairman.

Yoland   But who was the president at the time that they built the Lun On building? Who was responsible for the Lun On Co. and who were some of the men who were responsible for building those buildings?

Wally   It was controlled by the big shareholders. But the bottom line was still controlled by the On Leong Association.

Frank   You have to remember, back in those days, Chinese people had what we called social clubs. In those days Asian people couldn't get jobs so they got together and formed social clubs. As a matter fact, you know how you have these union banks, well, it was something like that…every week you pay in so much—you might have thirty people pay in so much every week and whoever wants that money for that week will bid on that money, okay, and the money that they bid for, that money would be used to go into business like a laundry or a restaurant—they pay that interest. For example for every hundred dollars you bid like two dollars, so that two dollars is considered dividends for the other people, and that's how a lot of people invest. And they formed these so called union banks; they started these little banks back then to back up the gambling, going to business, building, and stuff like that. People come and invest money, and you ask who Lun On is…Lun On is just like the name of a company, it's not one specific person. If you look at the history of the migration of the Asian people coming into this country, you will notice mostly male people coming into this country, hardly any female at all; the lucky ones got their wives over later on. So what did the male have to do? There's nothing left but to get together and play mahjong, pai qu, cards, you know… and this becomes the social club.

Now let me explain how the On Leong association came into existence. The Chinese people are very cliquish. You might belong to the Wong family and you might belong to the Chin family and we might belong to the Soo Hoo and how many Soo Hoo's do you hear about… Not many. Let's say the Wong family becomes very powerful and there are a lot of Wongs here, the Chin family also is very powerful, because they have a lot of Chins here. The Soo Hoo might be weak because there are only a few of us; in other words they gang together against you like; and lot of times back in those days you have like family feuds like the McCoy's against the Hatfields. You know, one of those things. Now On Leong Association was to put a stop to all that, you know. On Leong was going to represent all the minority family names; anybody is free to join. This was done to stop one group from dominating. For example, I can be a Soo Hoo and I can open up a restaurant or a laundry and I am doing very good, you know, maybe a Wong or a Chin family says, 'Hey, look, that guy is doing good, let's open up another laundry down the block and take the business away and under sell them. The Chin family or the Wong family would back them up, whoever it is, and put that guy out of business. In other words the minority family didn't have a chance, and the On Leong Association was to put a stop to all that. That was how this all got started. So all these associations back then, when they started, was all meant to be good.

Wally   Well, I know how that association was created. My uncle was the George Washington of the On Leong Association.

Yoland   What was his name?

Wally   Soo Hoo Mei Tong

Yoland   M - A - I?

Wally   Mai…you can say that, because it's just a pronunciation.

Yoland   And he was from China?

Wally   He was from China; he came to the U.S. around the same age as I did. He was about ten or twelve. He had a laundry with his uncle.

Yoland   Did he come straight to Newark Chinatown or did he go to…?

Wally   No, he came to Newark Chinatown once in a while, but he was in New York. Now during that time he was working in a laundry with his uncle. Some big family tried to get him out of the laundry and take over the laundry and he put up a fight for it. I think he must have hurt one of the fellows very bad. They arrested him; they put him in reform school.

Yoland   This is in the U.S., in New York?

Wally   Yes, in New York. They put him in reform school. When he came out of reform school he still had that grudge on those people who took the laundry. He said, "I won't let them get away with it." Then he started that association, he built that On Leong…. *On,* that means peace, *'Leung* is good…good peace…so a lot of minorities like us—Soo Hoo, Lee—Lee is a big family too—lots of small families, they all join in for protection. One time the big families start to squeeze the younger ones, they had to fight. They had a big fight with the Chin family in New York. They beat the Chin family, and then the Chin family couldn't fight with the On Leong because On Leong got all kind of minority families as members. You don't know if someone is an On Leong member or not. But if you are Chin, they call you a Chin they know you are a Chin, they hit you, and so eventually the Chin's gave up; that's when On Leong became powerful. New York On Leong association was the main branch.

Frank   You heard about the *tong* wars, that's like part of the *tong* wars, like one family against another family, all right, but this was the On Leong against the Chin family, because the Chin in New York at that time was a powerful, very strong family, they controlled everything.

Yoland   What about the Hip Sing? How did they come into the picture?

Frank   The Hip Sing is a spin off from New York.

Wally   Newark had a Hip Sing Association, but they had only two stores, past Market, near the Passaic River somewhere.

Yoland   Near Raymond Blvd?

168

Wally   I remember that. They weren't as powerful as the On Leong.

Yoland   I figured from Raymond Blvd to Market was Hip Sing and from Market down Mulberry to the other side was On Leong.

Wally   Yes.

Yoland   Now, how did the Hip Sing come to Newark?

Wally   They saw On Leong booming, gambling, booming, everything booming, lots of people in Newark, so they tried to get in.

Frank   You have to remember, every organization has to survive, and in order to survive you need money, so one of the ways of getting money is protection. If you noticed, every ethnic group that migrates to this country has their own, what you call, *Mafioso* group—now the Russians have it very big in this country. Back then the Chinese came in but they kept it within their own—the Cubans have that down in Miami, now the Russians have it in New York. It's something every ethnic group coming in here had. And to make the organization survive they had to go into collecting money—they need money. And the fastest way to do this is among your own people; they pay for protection and stuff like that.

Yoland   Did the Hip Sing have gambling rooms as well as laundries?

Wally   They all depended on them.

Yoland   So if the Hip Sing is between Market and Raymond what was it like on that side of town?

Wally   So slow, you hardly see a person, when you walk by you see a couple heads stick out the window.

Frank   Remember, you have to be loyal. The Hip Sing members will go to the Hip Sing side and gamble; the On Leong members would go to the On Leong side and gamble. Then you got these people that don't belong to any one organization and you find that a lot of gamblers are superstitious. If I can't win in this place, I'll go somewhere else and gamble and they go from place to place and gamble.

Wally   You know, during that time, New York Hip Sing was only about four or five stores. Most of the trouble that started between the two associations was caused by gambling, very seldom anything else. I think eighty percent by gambling, by cheating or stuff like that or robbery or something like that. On Leong strictly controlled all the business because my uncle made a law. He said to everybody if they have a restaurant on this corner, you know, no one can squeeze them out, because On Leong will protect them. If you want to open a restaurant, east, north, west, south, you got to leave at least one hundred numbers before you can open.

Frank   In other words, I am one forty five Mulberry Street. You want to open something near one forty, you've got to go to two forty five before you can open, you'd be quite a distance away from me, so you aren't competing with me and try to kill my business.

Wally   No matter how much money you spend, you cannot open. If you open they're going to do something. That's a law.

Frank   Back in those days, you have something that's booming and someone else that has money comes and opens up right next to you, steals half of your business and pretty soon, one of you is going to go down; and if you don't have a lot of money you are going to be the first one to go down, and they then survive and they take over all the business.

Yoland   Now both On Leong and Hip Sing had laundries right?

Wally   Yes.

Frank   Back in those days you had to remember there's no one that's going to hire an Asian. Most Asians they banded together to open up a restaurant just to survive, to have a job. Or they opened up a laundry. If you are by yourself, you might get together maybe with a brother or a cousin, and open up a laundry which is the cheapest business to go into. Back then, in the laundry business, I would say most were living in back of the laundry also. It was their place of residence and a place of business.

Back then, who's going to hire you? There's nothing for the Asian people to do except to go onto the laundry business. If there's a few of you and you don't have much money, the ones with a little more money put it together and open up a restaurant, because it costs more money to open up a restaurant.

Yoland   What were the restaurants in the Hip Sing area? Were there any on that side of Market Street?

Wally   No, there were only two stores there. They were gambling houses. How many laundries or something we don't know, because they were On Leong membership.

Yoland   Did the Hip Sing own restaurants?

Wally   All restaurants were On Leong.

Yoland   So the only thing the Hip Sing had was the gambling?

Wally   That's all they relied on. That's how they can survive. Half a year they have to close up and run away.

Yoland   New York is different?

Wally   New York is different—New York is a big Chinatown. New York's only Hip Sing was gambling in five stores on Doyer Street.

Frank   It's the same thing in New York. Certain streets belong to Hip Sing; certain streets belong to On Leong.

Yoland   When you were growing up and you came to this country and you became aware of the Chinatown, which Chinatown was larger, what was the difference between New York Chinatown and Newark Chinatown?

Wally   New York Chinatown was always larger. Newark Chinatown depended on New York Chinatown. People came over from New York Chinatown even when I was small. Because of the gambling, ninety percent of people came from New York.

Yoland   So Newark had no rules about gambling—it was not illegal to gamble in Newark?

Frank   It was illegal to gamble anywhere, but when the police buckled down on New York, all the gamblers would run to New Jersey to gamble, and when New Jersey knuckled down on Newark Chinatown, then all the gamblers would run to New York and gamble; so back and forth, depending on when the police department tightened up.

Wally   Mayor La Guardia was the best mayor in New York at that time. He stopped gambling in New York; that's why Newark was booming. They had a Catholic Church on Mott Street in New York and every year at a certain time, they were gambling by themselves. They say it was for the church, and its fine, but if a Chinese makes a mahjong game they complain to the police. They come down and close you up—that's why Chinese came to Newark. When Mayor LaGuardia was the mayor of New York, Newark was a booming town during those years.

Yoland   Now who was the mayor in Newark who cracked down on all the gambling, or who was the police commissioner who cracked down on all the gambling?

Wally   Newark police used to be run by mayor in the beginning of the 1920s; since then they changed, run by commissioner.

Yoland   Who was the mayor, do you remember?

Wally   Gee, I don't know the name. I was too young; I don't pay attention. That time when I was talking about Charlie King, he was the "Mayor of Chinatown," he controlled everything. I didn't know who he was or what he did, I don't know. But they considered him the Mayor for Chinatown.

Yoland   Now according to the research that I did, there was a time when there were three thousand Chinese in Newark, and this was supposed to be in the 1920s and 1930s?

Wally   These times was in the twenties. But, I remember 1929 or 1930, I began to have my restaurant, the Shanghai Restaurant on Mulberry Street; during that time the Chinatown was slowing down, either by the Depression or whatever it is, I don't know, but it began to be very hard to have a job. Newark was still a boom town, a nice good city. There were four, five movie houses, and all that sort of thing, two big restaurants on Broad Street; one was called Palace Royal and the other one was called Palais

Joi, right opposite the Old First Church; and another one was called Globe, which was way down right opposite the Robert Treat Hotel, where Military Park is located, right next to Haynes department store.

Yoland   When you say right next to Haynes, you mean on the same side of the street as Haynes.

Wally   Yes.

Yoland   First floor or second floor?

Wally   Second floor.

We look at pictures of 202 Mulberry.

Frank   Downstairs here was the Long Bar—down here on the main floor, and the Sai Woo restaurant was on this floor right here.

Yoland   But the bar wasn't Chinese.

Frank   No.

Yoland   They were renting from the Chinese owner?

Frank   Wallace? When did the Long Bar move into this building?

Wally   When the gambling all closed down.

Frank   Then the building was sold.

Wally   Yes, after the gambling was closed down, there was no more money and the building was sold.

Frank   When I was born, Newark Chinatown was already going downhill; there wasn't anything much of Newark Chinatown left.

Wally   At that time I sold my restaurant too.

Frank   This Long Bar club used to be the On Leong social club. Then the building was sold to some Jewish owners.

Wally   The Company was called Wolf.

Frank   They bought the building and they rented the first floor out to a bar called the Long Bar.

Yoland   So you're saying that 204 Mulberry, on the first floor, the business floor, what was the first business that was in there?

Frank   A social club.

Yoland   Did it have a name?

Frank   The Lun On, they owned this whole building.

Yoland   So it was the Lun On social club on the first floor, Sai Woo restaurant on the second floor, and you lived on the third.

Frank   And the rest of these floors were all Chinese residents. There are like three apartments on each floor, and after the building was sold the social club was then rented out to the Long Bar.

Yoland   Now at that time when the gambling ended and Wolf took over the building, was that around the time when most of the Chinese people were leaving Chinatown, or were the majority of the people already in New York?

Frank   You have to remember, the laws and rules in Newark Chinatown are starting to change. There is always a reason why they are leaving Newark Chinatown. From what I heard ninety percent of Newark Chinese were here illegally and most of them would survive from gambling and everything and the police department in Newark started to take mug shots whenever they raided and you were caught for gambling. And people were thinking, "Hey, I'm here illegally, I don't want my picture taken. Immigration might get a hold of it and deport me and take me back." So a lot of these people started moving to New York instead.

Yoland   What about the raids?

Wally   Back then, when you get raided in gambling, you pay a fine and they let you go.

Yoland   Were there a lot of raids?

Wally   Oh yes, day and night.

Frank   They'd fill up a paddy wagon—when we were kids we used to watch them pull up a paddy wagon and then march the people onto the paddy wagon take them down to the police headquarters, book them, and a couple hours later you'd see them out on the street talking. Back then they were like always raiding the gambling joints—lock them up they pay the fine and then they all come out.

Yoland   I read in the newspaper that one year there were fifty-two raids. I read how the raids took place—and you can tell me if this is correct—the newspaper says they came with axes and chopped down people's houses.

Wally   And doors....

Yoland   Do you remember any of that?

Wally   Well, yeah....

Yoland   Tell me about that; tell me what you remember.

Frank   They chopped up their door, they chopped up their gambling tables...

Wally   He was too young to remember Harry Li Sooey, the younger, but that was his father's place they chopped up, and when he came out from jail, he started lying to the people in Chinatown. He said, "I'm going to have the okay to operate gambling." A lot of people asked me if what he said was true or false. I said false—I don't think we can operate—I don't think anybody can operate. Now I know the whole town in Newark. I know all the mob people, not only the Chinese people, Italians, Jewish all colored people. I know that the whole city was in a bottleneck tight, nobody can operate. I know that.

Yoland   What year was that?

Wally   This was around about 1944 or 1945.

Yoland   So this was after the raids of the thirties.

Wally   Yeah, after the thirties. At this time Newark Chinatown started to be reborn again, in the forties, because New York Chinatown, you can open one day and close down the next day. So people in Newark like Harry Li Sooey, the elder, said he's going to open. He asked me if I hear that it's okay to open; I say I don't hear anything. I don't think it's a good idea; so he operated anyway. What information he had I don't know because I know a lot of people in Newark. I'm a hustler too because I was pushing around, nobody would hire me on a job, I got to hustle because my father was too old to work. I remember Harry Li Sooey asks me to be a share with his gambling and I talked to him personally, he said, "Wallace, I'm going to open." I said to him, "I don't think anybody can open at this time"—you know why, because it's election time.

Yoland   Election time in Newark?

Wally   In Newark. He said, "No, no, I'm okay." So, I say, "I don't want any part of it. You want to do it; you do it on your own." He said, "Well, you don't have to show up; I'll put you on the pay roll"—I still say, "No, cut me out completely"—and I knew because I checked up on his information and I found out from one of the Jewish racketeers. He said, "What is he crazy?" He also told him not to open, nobody can open. So finally Li Sooey opened. The second day the police commissioner and his gang comes with the hammer, breaks everything down.

Yoland   What was the name of the police commissioner?

Wally   I think that time it was Commissioner Cash or something like that.

Yoland   What year was that?

Wally   I think it was the forties, 1944 or 1945. They cracked down, break the table, and all that was on the table they take it away.

Yoland   Where was that? What store was that?

Wally   The store right on the second floor of the standard restaurant, upstairs.

Yoland   Is that what used to be the Filipino club, at one time the second floor
          of the Pinto building?

Wally   Yes. That was the Standard Restaurant.

Frank   Back in those days it was a common thing for the police to come down
          and raid, and naturally nobody want to open the door for them. In there,
          you've got gambling tables and everything. They had to break down
          the door to go in. Once they are in there, the first thing they do is chop
          up the gambling tables so you don't have it anymore. This is like an
          actual thing, like in the movies, the roaring twenties. In the movies they
          come in there, they break down the door. Hey, I'm not going to try to
          let you in. They try to hide everything first, meanwhile the cops are
          breaking the door down; you're trying to hide something while they
          are chopping up your table. It was a normal thing.

Wally   The main thing is they want to put the money away in their pocket first.
          Remember all policemen, regardless of where they are, where they
          come from, the first thing they do when they go in, they grab the
          money.

Yoland   For their pocket or for evidence?

Wally   I don't know...I don't know...you can imagine yourself. If I tell you
          everything from my experience in Chinatown, boy, they were so
          crooked. I was in Chinatown for over twenty years before he was born.

Yoland   But you were a teenager?

Wally   But I'm smart.

Yoland   You were a hip teenager.

Wally   I'm a hustler, because my father he died and I have a sister and a brother
          to look after.

LOOKING FOR CHINATOWN ~ 7

Aunt Fanny and Uncle Nat

My uncle Nathaniel was Chinese, and like many Chinese from
Trinidad he had a colonial British name. He came to America
before my family immigrated and made a fortune here gambling.
Then like all the other immigrant men he eventually brought my
aunt Fanella (Fanny for short), daughter and two sons, to Brooklyn to a second floor apartment overlooking Flatbush Avenue.
This was a swanky place at that time. All the Brooklyn Dodgers
lived in the neighborhood. My uncle was always amazing to me.
He was very handsome, with his black hair swept back without
a part, shining and never a hair out of place, like Clark Gable in
"Gone with the Wind." He was a happy-go-lucky fellow who
laughed comfortably, played with and was always friendly to us
kids, loved his beautiful wife and children dearly and would not
let them want for anything, and they lived in middle-class luxury, all from his gambling. He and my father were very good
friends and I can hear them laughing together now in the happy
atmosphere of his house. The rest of the family struggled to
keep their heads above water wishing and looking to my aunt
and uncle as leaders in the family of what life in America should
be. My cousin, also named Fanny, had all the latest comic
books, wore the most stylish teen girl clothes, had a record
player in her room with the latest rock and roll records and her
walls were decorated with movie stars pictures and boyfriends
college football pennants. I spent a lot of time in her room feeling

like a deprived teen, wishing I could be like Fanny. When his eldest son Anthony was seventeen, he had a red Chevy Corvette. We went out for a drive and I hoped all my friends could see us and think he was my boyfriend. I was a girl of sixteen, and he was as handsome as his father. How my uncle succeeded so well at gambling (specifically horse racing) is a mystery to me. But then, he had nothing to lose; he was an immigrant in a society that saw him as second-class citizen who had no education and no chance of making anything of himself except to be a laborer with no future, no way to achieve the American dream. Unlike my father, he was not going to work himself to an old age only to get just a taste. He went after it all.

PART 7

ON GAMBLING

I

The Mayor Takes a Stand—

Gambling and Economics

On May 9, 1890, Mayor Haynes of Newark attempted to speak in a court hearing in defense of twenty-six Chinese men who were arrested for gambling. It seems that a neighbor complained that there was a lot of noise coming from the house of Sam Lee at 12 Fair Street. The police arrived at 1:00 A.M. and, standing across the street from the house on the south side of Fair Street, heard the sound of men talking loudly in Chinese and attempted to enter the front of the building, but the door was locked, so they went around to the rear and were admitted by a Chinese man. The men had been gambling and as they did so, their discussions got heavy and they began to argue.

They were arrested and taken to jail and allowed no counsel. The next morning at their hearing the mayor was protesting against the illegality of the interrogations as they were proceeding. The judge threatened the mayor and reminded him that he had no standing in the judge's court. The mayor left and returned with counsel for the men but was ridiculed by the police, stating that he had sympathies for the Chinese. The mayor's last statement to the court is very interesting. He stated to the policemen and the judge, "If you want to distinguish yourself, you should go to the Essex Club, where hundreds of dollars change hands daily." The Essex Club, then located at 44 Park Place, was at this time a place for the wealthy Newark businessmen and social set to gamble, smoke, do business and carouse in gentlemanly fashion.

Taken from the Newark Evening News, May 9, 1890
    Hostility toward minority groups, whether you call it racism,

bigotry, or nationalism, seems to be an intrinsic part of the American way of life. From its colonial beginnings, we see it woven into the fabric of the experiences of all who struggled to achieve what became known as the success of "the American Dream." Nothing has changed after centuries. Prior to the Chinese immigration, there were no laws preventing anyone from entering America. There were no limits in numbers, race, or class status. "All ye who enter here..." came through wide open gates. It was economics, and it has always been economics, that create the hostilities that still exist today. Each group wants a piece of the pie. It is as Darwin states "the survival of the fittest." But while at the same time there was hostility toward the ethnic groups in Newark, there was always the minority of those and specifically those with power who did stand up for the Chinese.

In 1869, a group of women shoe stitchers in Lynn, Massachusetts, organized the Daughters of St. Crispin, a national women's labor organization modeled on and supported by the Knights of St. Crispin, the national shoe workers union, which also went on record supporting equal pay for equal work. The Daughters of St. Crispin is recognized as the first national union of women. (Jone Johnson Lewis, *Women and Unions, Late 19th Century Labor Organizing by and for Women.* About.com Women's History, Issues and Events. Text copyright 1999-2006 © Jone Johnson Lewis)

When the Chinese arrived in Belleville, they replaced a group of mainly Irish workers in Hervey's laundry. The women had asked for raises and shorter working hours. Hervey refused, and brought in the Chinese. The women called on the Crispin Union to defend their rights to work. The racial friction this caused was part of the recurring hostility Chinese experienced until the twentieth century, and is part of the fabric of immigrant life in the U.S. From the beginning of the Chinese arrival in Newark, many community members, police, and some government organizations could not reconcile to the presence of the Chinese among them. The mainly Irish police department raided the Chinese establishments regularly, consistently increasing their take.

II

Gambling in Chinatown

In traditional societies without money, people may gamble with any commodity. In the civilized world, there is the stock market as a legitimate business enterprise, and the state lottery as a means of raising money for "worthy" causes. Gambling, if not inherent, is at least a universal human trait. The gambling impulse, in and of itself, is non moral and not immoral. There are, however, a small number of cases where gambling becomes immoral because it becomes excessive and goes beyond the limits of control by the person or because it brings misery and suffering to the person or to his family. But why do some individuals of certain social groups over-indulge in gambling?

There were several incidents of gambling fights recorded at the laundry in Belleville. As a matter of fact, one report has Hervey using the gambling by the Chinese as one of the reasons he decided to sell the laundry. American society has always had a double meaning for all of its laws. Gambling has always been seen as a negative practice by all American religious groups. This was not different in nineteenth century New Jersey, where anti-gambling laws did not exist. Legally, a man could not be put in jail for gambling, however, in many cases, the conservative views of the society were used against the Chinese as a way to harass them.

In his comments about his father, Bob Lee notes the relationship of the gambling to the attitude, or pose taken by a Chinese-American man. This attitude was similar to the one I saw in my uncle, an attitude that states, "I know what I am all about. And despite all the setbacks you present me I know where I can maneuver, and will maneuver there pushing any confines I can until they give way." There is an unconscious intuitiveness that the gambler uses, develops keenly as Bob's father did "...he would play mahjong at night, touch the tiles

185

with his thumb, know what they are without looking, make the right move, and risk his cash on the line." Bob stated.

In his analysis of his father and his father's gambling, Bob uses the word *risk*, but is there a risk when one is sure there is no other move; is this risk or reality? The term risk involves some meaning of hesitation, chance, question, but for these gamblers there was no risk because what they had was not a reality they could identify with, therefore they existed in an unknown world. The movement through life in the opium haze must have alleviated some of this unknown quantity from their mental view of their surroundings and their psychological inability to accept not being allowed to adapt and merge.

III

ON GAMBLING AND GROWING UP

Interview w/ Bob Lee (continued), Bob Lee's Analysis

Yoland   You talked about your father and gambling, and from my interviews, many of the Chinatown men gambled, some even ran gambling rooms. There was also talk about Ipaw's (the bean sprout lady's) house as being the place where Eng family members gathered to play mahjong. When did you become aware of your father's gambling?

Bob   Well first of all I don't know if my father ever went to Ipaw's house to gamble or play Mahjong. I do know that at some holidays families would gather there. As far as gambling, well think of it this way. You come to the U.S. thinking that you're going to pick gold up off the streets, which is one of the stories that is told to you to make you go into debt and get on this boat to come here, and you make promises to your family that you are going to send back some of this gold, and then you come here and find that you belong to a certain class that is on the bottom and you have to work harder than you worked in China and you are isolated from the rest of the society not only by class but also by language and culture, you have to find an outlet. The family associations whether you are an Eng, Wong, or Lee are all there is to help you integrate into the kind of enclave which protects you, because the larger society doesn't protect you. And so, Chinese men, the bachelor society, the men who came after the exclusion laws, responded in a certain way. They felt isolated, they felt discouraged, yet they still have their obli-

187

gations to send money to family back home. And sometimes they also have a family in this country, so I think that's how my father got involved, in his case, with playing the horses. I knew that he was gambling, and at one time he said that this was something he knew he was addicted to, and that the only way he could survive with this addiction was to become a bookie, and so he had a few bets that people would give him. I think I was old enough then to run across the street and buy things – that was the age when I knew he was taking bets. So that at some point he would hear of a great inside tip and instead of ironing the shirts or washing the clothes he would have taken off down to the track with his friends and my mother would complain about these kinds of things. So that's how it affected the family. Sometimes he would come back unapproachable and other times he would come back full of joy and he would give my mother some money and he would give us a few bucks. Those things happened once in a while, not that often. I think a lot of Asian men responded this way to life here. They were in a certain way isolated from their own wives because they had to deal with problems that they could not share with their own wives, or their wives could not understand, so the men did things together that were separate from their children, if not their whole family. I think the other question you asked me was about discrimination, class relationships and the only story I can remember about that is when my father's mother died and I was asking where is Papa, my mother told me not to bother him, that he was in the bedroom. Apparently he was in there and apparently he was crying and she just did not want me to go anywhere near there. But I never saw that, I just knew that he was in that room. It was around this time too that she told me that once during the war he had a job working in a factory to produce military stuff and the boss had said something to him which was apparently of some racist nature and it made him very upset. So I knew these few little touches, insights into what affected him, what was important to him, otherwise these were kept from us.

We were becoming American; they wanted us to learn English. They didn't try to teach us Chinese, we didn't speak Chinese at home. They were proud that we were going to have opportunities. We were going to get an education, so they did certain things, like not telling us about the old country. They wanted us to become part of the new country. Then suddenly one day they realized we were not speaking Chinese, they made efforts to try to get us to speak Chinese and my father would hold lessons in the laundry which my sister and I pooh-poohed. We were American, we were great, we were whatever, and so he quickly got frustrated with that. Eventually Mr. Mon set up a Chinese School in Old First Church and a group of us kids from other families got together and that went on for a year or so before they gave up on that. But they wanted us to get further than they got and they saw that to do these things – this was how you do it. They didn't want to tell us about their Chinese beliefs; they didn't want to tell us about Chinese religion or Chinese folk religion, if they knew anything about it. They didn't want us to know about what they considered their own superstitious beliefs. So when stories would come up at Mr. Mon's house and women would claim to see little children running around the table and talk about it and there were no little children there, but they would see them, these would be attributed to be ghosts. My father also told me that once he was sitting around a large water fountain in the town in China and asking somebody where everybody is because the village seemed empty, and I can't remember what this person said to him but apparently he understood that this person wasn't there. This was some kind of a ghost, so he had had some kind of an unusual experience too. But my parents did not want to tell us about beliefs that would alienate us from the society in which they were joining. They were very embarrassed about these things. One time I came back from school and my teacher had asked what religion are we, and my parents didn't know what to tell us, they couldn't answer. They said Oh, well we go to Old First Church and that's a Presbyterian church so just say you're that. The children in the community went there and my mother and father never went there. It wasn't until several years later working in New York Chinatown that I found the nature of Chinese folk religion; what it's like and how it's so syncretic. If my mother had gone to the deity in the temple in Toishan and prayed for a boy child, she never told me. But that is what she and the other young women in China may have done.

My father was a quiet person and quiet people sometimes have an awful lot to say and say to us. They say it to us in ways which may not be in words, but they occupy a very specific place in our sensibility. We feel we know them in some way, in a deeper way, than perhaps we know other people, and certainly he was that kind of person. My mother once said to us and would complain, "He expects us to read his mind," or "He expects me to read his mind," and she wasn't going to do that. So he did in many ways, he expected you to understand his situation in his silence, and when you didn't he seemed to size you up as to what kind of person you were because you were not able to communicate on that level. I think to a certain extent I've come to believe Chinese culture operates this way. Chinese culture operates in silence and silence is deeply religious, it's deeply spiritual, everybody understands silence in this way. To understand silence purely in its non-communicative aspect, in its reticent even anti-social form is to misunderstand what people are trying to say to us, and to communicate to us and to be for us in a culture in which words and language and verbosity is the way in which our legal system and our social system and our society functions, this society anyway. So, for me a major aspect of what I'm doing here in this place is to integrate two cultures that function on two different modalities. I mean I was being introduced into a culture in which I had to speak and speak well and write well and my mother was certainly very outgoing and people had a big admiration for my mother. She was that type of person; on the other hand, my father was this presence that I began to study. And it became more and more significant for me to understand his situation. He was not just this person who won some money on the track and my mother would refuse the money. She wouldn't have anything to do with it.

Once I was driving along in the car, this was when I was much older, and he's sitting next to me and he's watching me drive and he says, "You watch the white line, I watch the curb." And he was utterly right, I always find I drive on the right hand side and I watch the white line. So I said, "No, I don't watch the curb." I wouldn't know how to drive if I had to watch the curb, but certainly I understood that he was saying, that he had a sense of reality that I didn't. He had a sense of the consequences of bouncing into something physical that I didn't and that I had this sense of American law of what was right rather than what was *real*.

Yoland: What were some of the realities that you had to live through as a young Chinese American growing up in Newark Chinatown?

Bob: I wished my parents were willing to tell me things about China more so. 'Cause what happens is that without this kind of integration fully into your past and who you are and what you are, ...is something you want to know about. There is no place in your education through college, at least in the years that I was going to school, that would inform you of these things. So you're really handicapped in that way. My father wanted me to become an engineer.

Yoland: In terms of what you're saying, let's take it back to Newark Chinatown, let's take it back to the time when you're growing up there, when there are other families in Chinatown who you might have met at East Side High, or at Mr. Mon's or even at Lafayette Street School and they are all growing up as Chinese American. What were their realities at that time?

Bob: My sisters' generation was more a part of the aftermath of World War II. A lot of these guys had been in the military, whether they actually saw action in World War II or in the Korean War, I don't know. But I know that they expressed their masculinity by this willingness to participate in the military, to walk around proudly with military uniforms, to do things that were American, like go bowling every Thursday night, or play a hard game of basketball every week, also on Thursday night. These were a group of guys who were tough and strong. A few of them were driving around in convertibles and making it with the girls. So I think that the generation was in part coming out of that time when you were on the winning side, you were American. You were Chinese; you were not Japanese, so you were not in the camps. You had integrated into the American community. And so being able to participate in the military was part of that. There was no term or place for anybody like myself, who wanted to claim a social difference, a different posture. The term "Asian American" didn't come about until '69, I think before 1970, when we would get together and talk about what we wanted to call ourselves. We were demonstrating in Chinatown. We came to Chinatown to help our community, to help their community. Therefore, we were willing to be assertive.

Yoland: But there must have been a transition, a transition from wanting to be a part of the American dream and wanting to be Asian American. When did that occur for you, what was the reality that woke you up to 'I want to be Asian American.' When did you leave Newark Chinatown? How did you get to New York Chinatown? Why Chinatown, why not the suburbs?

Bob: I think a lot of what I have been expressing is all about this kind of existence, which is fragmented and dislocated. Newark was an experience for me that never hung together, never made any sense, never gave me any sense of the fundamental questions. So that while going to college, these things were still not there. So it's in the streets, demonstrating for civil rights, demonstrating against the war, that you find that you have camaraderie and something in common with other people. They felt similarly disfranchised or dislocated and certain grievances came out and we were able to proclaim them as a kind of positive presence.

Yoland: I spoke to several other people of your generation; they all went to work for General Electric, General Motors, various other corporate structures. They fit into a very typical American mainstream life; you didn't. How many other Newark Chinatown people broke away?

Bob: I don't really have an answer for you on this. All I can tell you is that I had an artistic sensibility, that I had a lot of questions when I was growing up. I knew I didn't want to become an engineer. There were enough engineers in the world. I had a situation in which my father, my family, didn't need me to earn money for them, so I had this chance to be independent and pursue certain questions and if I didn't have a good income or if I didn't have a retirement fund that didn't matter. For me the movement, the Asian-American movement, was a way for me to link up my understanding of the arts to the social and political situation of the Asian-American Community and to see that as a way of turning it into a viable project. A project that could garner means by which to earn a living was one of the ways in which this happened.

Yoland   Going back to Newark Chinatown; what are some of the things that you hold dear when you think about Newark Chinatown?

Bob   I don't have any of those. Newark Chinatown was the place where I grew up. This was part of my reality. I don't have any favorite things. I have memories of what it was like. I don't think a lot about it, sometimes I wish I did. I hear people say, Oh this is their favorite desert, or this is their favorite game or this is their favorite movie or this is their favorite actor. I don't have any of these favorite things because it's all been very dead pan and I guess my impression of the whole culture is that it's a lot of people who immigrated to this country who have lost something vital to them and what preoccupies us today, celebrities, materialism are not something that feeds us deeply on any level.

    Actually, there's a couple of things, like visiting Ipaw, stopping over once in awhile to the restaurant where Norma and Segat were, stopping over in the Kee Chee grocery store, or places like that once in awhile, going to Peter Hong's house to see his mother. But mostly Peter

Hong and I would go to Branch Brook to play around in the city's empty lots. There were these different things.

The other thing that I want to mention to you is that Asian men were being handicapped by the society and being considered less masculine so that they were not a threat. Whereas the women were being seen as exotic, erotic, these were the basic stereotypes of Asian males and females of America in the fifties and sixties. Women were not as handicapped as Asian men were, and the women were able to take advantage of that to the extent that they were the strength of the family. They really held the family together. They had a love and strength and a sense of positiveness that they were trying to give to their children, to see them through this difficult time; the same difficult time that they could see their husbands were going through; that their community was going through. And yet they could put aside their grievances and offer the strength that they had every day, every moment, and I saw this in my own mother, I see this in other mothers. Chinese mothers did this for their family.

Yoland: Did you know Norma Eng Wong very well?

Bob: I knew Norma had a different kind of family that we did. I saw her with her kids next to the piano all singing together, these American songs. I saw that she retained a certain kind of moral, a certain kind of spirit, a certain kind of energy, tenacity and strength and in many ways I didn't think of it in those days but I certainly think of it now as how remarkable. Given the conditions that she lived with - that this is a very small Chinese community and yet you maintain this level of vitality in your family, in your community. Given that you go out the door and there's a whole different world going on. So now I understand how remarkable these things are and how much women today need to understand what they are taking on when they start a family.

Interview with Bob Lee, July 3, 2002

Bob   I remember my father walking around Newark Chinatown, acting macho in a way only Chinese men act macho. He would wait his moment, project when his horse might come in, and take a leap when he thought the time had come. Or he would play mahjong at night, touch the tiles with his thumb, know what they are without looking, make the right move, and risk his cash on the line. A gambler, he knew what he had on the line. He was clear headed in this way. Much was on the line that he did not know, could not know, or had no tools to manipulate and transform those indecipherable feelings that had no adequate words, no expression that was commensurate to the import of what those feelings carried. Yes, he got upset, flared up, impatient with what he could not do or grasp, but he lived with those feelings, felt them, and stayed true to them.

He knew what was on the line each day, each moment in ways I find myself lacking with all my words and concepts and intellectuality. I'm not aware, moment to moment, what I risk, what's at stake, and that creates obstacles to the flow of how I wish to spend my life in the fullness and richness of what it could be.

Interview with Bob Lee, July 28, 2002

Bob: I was more aware of the peculiarities of people in Newark than I may have been of my own difference from others; that came later. I did not grow up as the boys in my sister's generation. I did not have a brother or a continuum of close friends so I had no coherent social context to serve as a norm. My sensitivities led me to perceive things no one else saw, so with no one to share them I became more alone with my own musings. As a child I drew pictures of the people who entered my father's hand laundry on Court St. across from the 1st Police Precinct. Sylvia collected those drawings, a variety of potato heads with tiny features each different, each unique. Little did I know I was one of those potato heads who would stick out in public school as a conspicuous and unusual curiosity. As my drawings became more ambitious, I drew a large replica of the head of Alfred E. Neumann on poster paper saying, "What, me worry? I bring my laundry here," and placed it in our shop window. The lost souls who wandered around Newark and found themselves before the court of dirty clothes would not sadden me; it was innocence's madness to remain cheerful in the face of such desolation. I took my mama's joy and delight before nature daily, though the streets of this U.S. inner city had somehow fused itself to the trees and soil. She kept her Chinese village soul, as much for herself as for her children. I loved to play behind the houses just below High Street where the soil rose like a mountain. Children would play in summer weeds and in winter down snowy slopes. Often in war games, we would form teams; one would hide and trap, while the other would seek them out. I would make the toy rifles for most, warehouse them, and hand them out when it came time to play.

The first association of myself with that called Chinese and China was when I was told not to play too far around the corner, I had to take care and could not go where the other boys might go. I was somehow not like them, and my potato head curiosity began my musings about what it meant to be colored, why others did not feel what I felt, see what I saw, what was it to be like my mom, my father, my relatives and those in what seemed far away Chinatown on Mulberry Street. This was where my shame for not speaking Chinese was pointed out regularly, where what I came to know as Chinese was this tiny isolated back water enclave that was to be put aside before the dynamic, the forward looking and fair minded, those with a future. I wanted to be that, I was going to prove I could be American. I attuned myself to speaking and writing English well. It was not till leaving college, after learning about art, about China's Bronze Age ethics, and watching the social upheavals that decimated the downtown area of Newark that I accepted the idea that I would never be around people speaking a Chinese language I could never fully understand.

33-The Globe Restaurant, a Chinese American Restaurant on Broad near Central, circa late 1800's, Cone Collection, courtesy NJ Historical Society.

32- Young Bob Lee and his family at a Chinatown restaurant, late 1940's, courtesy Bob Lee.

34- Gladys Eng Chin and family at Palais Joy Restaurant on Broad Street, courtesy Gladys Eng Chin.

35-Norma and husband, See Gat Eng Wong at Shaighai Restaurant on Mulberry Street, which they owned during 40's thru 60's, courtesy Bob Lee.

36-Mulberry Street in heart of Newark Chinatown with Shanghai Restaurant on left, circa 1930's, courtesy Robert Steinbaum, Law Journal.

LOOKING FOR CHINATOWN · 8

About Restaurants

In Newark Chinatown there were no children playing on the streets until probably the early fifties, definitely in the sixties and then it was on weekends only. Not to say there were no children who lived there until that time, but that the children who were there, who were old enough to be on the street playing, were working in their family businesses or in businesses owned by other members of the community. Children worked. Joe Young arrived in Newark at age thirteen and immediately started working in his father's laundry. Bob Lee's father also came as a young man and started working immediately in his father's laundry. Victor Fong worked in his mother's restaurant, and met his wife there in the sixties. Paul Eng Wong, also a child of the sixties, remembers being seven years old and working in his mother and father's restaurant which was on Mulberry Street. Frank Eng remembers being a young boy and working in the Chinese restaurants on Broad Street.

Chinese restaurants are what everyone remembers about Newark Chinatown; even Chinese people remember this. The generation that is still alive today speaks of big restaurants on Broad Street that hosted the Big Bands live, with dancing and excellent Chinese American food, cheap. This was a symbol of Chinatown's success.

My mother and father never took us to a restaurant. I never ate out until I went to college. When I worked at Woolworth during my summer vacations, my mother and I brought our lunch.

We would sometimes buy a cup of tea at Woolworth's cafeteria but that was the extent of eating out. During the school year, after school my friends and I would hang out at the pizza parlor, but that was the extent of my venture into the world of eating out. You had to have money to eat out, and why should we eat out when my mother always cooked and she was such a great cook. I don't even recall mention of talk about Chinese restaurants until I returned to Trinidad in 1963 and was taken to one by my uncle, who pointed out to me that the food was a mixture of Chinese and Creole.

When I researched the historical archives, I found only two photos of Chinese restaurants in Newark yet there were so many more. I found photos of restaurants that were not marked "Chinese", but when I examined the interior scenes I recognized Chinese utensils and knew they were interiors of Chinese restaurants. What happened to all these restaurants? Why did they leave, some for the suburbs, some for New York City, all gone forever?

Recently I got a couple of photographs from the New Jersey Historical Society and they wanted to know if I knew anything about them. The photos were obviously Chinese restaurants in Newark. One was an interior labeled by the photographer to have been in Newark, the other I was able to research, an exterior scene with other businesses around it. I found that it existed on Broad Street in Newark and the physical building still existed.

The picture showed the exterior of the restaurant and it was obvious from the clothing the people wore that it was a thriving and important social setting. The people were very well dressed and the physical décor of the restaurant was very 1920s chic. Many of the restaurants at this time had French names, but they were Chinese restaurants, and according to Frank Eng, the Chinese chefs were trained in French cooking and many dishes were French as well as Chinese. By the time I came to Newark, they had all disappeared. Even the last remnant of the old days, Ding Ho, had been renamed and taken over by Mr. Yang who later sold it and the named changed again to Heng Sheng. The Heng Sheng, still stands on Green Street, it has a different name now, the only remnant of a Chinatown that was. The ghosts of Newark Chinatown are being driven away and soon all will be forgotten.

Interview with Norma Eng Wong and George and May Eng

Yoland: What years were your most prosperous in the restaurant?

Norma: Before the war and after the war, because during the war....

George: There was the ration.

Yoland: What was the ration like? Was it different for Chinese?

Norma: No, not the ration, the customers. You can't have black customers coming up—you have to shake your head and they know—all you have to say is sorry.

Yoland: You were not allowed during the war to have black customers? How come, who—how could they have a law like that?

Norma: They would look up and see the headwaiter and if the headwaiter said no, they would leave. But after the war you had to let everybody in. After the war we have a lot of black customers. Because they said now you have to say yes to everybody.

Yoland: Was this for the whole city?

Norma: Yes! There was another Chinese restaurant all the way down near the post office parking lot, which was a restaurant that served only colored trade, can't even think of their name. It was about two or four stores away from Mrs. Fong. So it was like number 222.

Yoland: Mrs. Fong owned the Canton.

Norma: No they owned a restaurant but I don't know the name.

Yoland: Well I'm going to take more pictures of the neighborhood and maybe you could point out these places.

Norma: There was a cute little restaurant, it had two little
dining rooms, it was a brick house, and it had two
entrances, one door goes into one entrance and another goes into the other entrance to the back. I
think that was the Canton, they served colored trade
in the back.

The Bean Sprout Lady
I first heard about the bean sprout lady from Norma Eng Wong.
Norma was telling me about the people in the neighborhood
whom she found most incredible. When she spoke about the
bean sprout lady, her voice got excited and she was experiencing
the same amazement she experienced when she was in the
neighborhood talking with or looking at the bean sprout lady.
The bean sprout lady's name was Jean, but she was also called
in Chinese Ipaw by those who knew her well. She lived at 81
Columbia Street, a turn of the century one-family home which
had been converted into apartments, one on each floor. Last year
the house was for sale and I had an opportunity to examine the
entire house and the basement where the bean sprouts were
grown. The upper part of the house looked like most of the other
houses that had been converted. The old banister rail was the
same simple wooden style that most of these working class
houses had. The basement was very unusual however, because
it seemed to be dug out of the ground. It wasn't very deep and
the walls, though brick, had a feeling as though someone had
taken a shovel and dug the entire space. In the middle of the
floor was a new furnace. Obviously this was not here when the
bean sprout lady grew her beans sprouts here. I looked around
the room imagining how she may have grown her bean sprouts
in this cramped space. It definitely was dark and you needed
dark for bean sprouts to grow. You also needed moisture so there
may have been a sink down here or she may have brought water
down from the first floor.
    After the first time I heard about Jean, it seemed that every-
one I spoke to had an image of her in their minds. Some remem-

bered her huge station wagon in which she drove around, and from which she would pull the crates of bean sprouts, and climb the stairs carrying her crates of bean sprouts to the restaurants. Others remembered her house as a meeting place for playing Mahjong. A place where all the game playing members of the community who were part of that clique would gather for all night gaming, or gaming for days. They would order food from the restaurants and just keep playing. The people I interviewed who were my age were children when she lived there, and they remembered going to her house during holidays to have holiday celebrations. The families went at Christmas and probably other times too. They remembered playing with the other children at her house. Jean was about 4 feet tall and very thin and wiry. She had had a bout with cancer and had survived. Her youngest son was not so lucky however, he died, but no one remembers the cause. Her daughter is supposed to be still alive somewhere in the Midwest where she moved after her mother died. She had gone to college there and opted to stay there and live. Life there was not as hard and unsafe as in Newark. As I researched more and more of the names of the people in Newark Chinatown, I found many people who may have been related to Jean. They had the same clan name, and in some cases the names were so similar that I thought I may have found the same person with different name changes. Jean was an Eng, although she did not carry the Eng surname, but I found information that showed she was related to Charlie King and may have been related to Chinese persons that are dated to have been in Newark in the 1800s. I found photos of Jean at the beach with her daughter and another family, and I will always remember Norma's amazement as she spoke of Jean, the bean sprout lady, as she is now referred to by those I interview.

I then sent an email to my friend Iris Torres who now owns the house of the 'bean sprout lady,' Jean Eng. At the time, Iris was currently stationed at one of the Air Force bases in Afghanistan. When I first met her she had just returned from her tour in Iraq. When she was in Iraq, she often sent me photographs of her life there and the planes she flew in, and the places she visited. Iris is a good photographer.

*Saturday, November 01, 2003 - Emails sent to my friend Iris
Tores.*

Iris,

Did you know that your house on 81 Columbia was once owned
by a Chinese lady who grew bean sprouts in the basement and
sold them to the Chinese restaurants? Do you remember who
you bought the house from? Try to remember when you were a
kid who lived there? Were there any Chinese there then and in
the neighborhood?

Yoli

Hi Yoli,

Yep, I remember the Chinese lady who owned the house, but
I can't remember her name...I do remember what she looks
like, and she also had a daughter who was very nice and intelligent... she sold the house because was getting old and her
daughter wanted her to move in...I remember she used to have
a Doberman Pincher who actually was the daughter's and was
well trained...there were some other Chinese in the neighborhood too. Why??

Iris

Iris,

Great, this lady grew bean sprouts in her basement and was a
very important part of Newark Chinatown. Try to remember
everything you can about her in the next few days and when you
remember something email it to me. Do you remember where
she moved to? How would you describe her psychically, and her
daughter too? This is very important because I am writing a book
about the Chinatown.

Yoli

What I remember about her physique is: she was about 5'
tall...thin...always wore black...I think she was a widow...she had
black hair and as the years went by she was becoming gray....she
kept a lot to herself. However, before my dad bought the
house...she used to talk to my mom a lot...her daughter was very
friendly...I think she was in her thirties at the time...she was
about 5'4"...nicely built...her daughter did marry, but I have no
clue to where...plus, she had the dobby dog....

Iris
Do you remember seeing when she had people over to her house on Christmas or whenever and keep trying to remember little things as you go through your day. Did you know anybody else Chinese in the neighborhood. How old were you then?

Yoli
I was a kid...about 7 yrs. old...I don't remember if she had people over her house...I do remember that maybe she might have rented rooms to Chinese folks...the other Chinese person was down the block...there was a house next to 75 Columbia Street where an old Chinese man use to live...then Jimmy's dad was Chinese...he lived in the basement on 69 Columbia Street...plus up the block three houses from the Cigar Store is the other Chinese house...but I have no clue of those folks...I can't tell you much for I didn't pay too much mind to the Chinese folks...when you're at that age, all you think about is playing...
Iris

Iris
Thanks so much for that info...keep your mind open and if you come across any stories or anything let me know. Did you know the restaurants that were on Mulberry Street?
Yoli

No, I really don't remember the names of the restaurants...I do know that on Mulberry Street, right next to the tavern...Chinese folks ran the deli...at the time, it was called Young's or Young's Deli...the father ran the store and then the son/daughter worked it at times...
Iris

Do you remember Wah Hing Grocery on Mulberry or Canton Restaurant on corner of Green and Mulberry, or maybe Ding Ho Restaurant on Green. Going to walk the dog now. Y
I do remember Canton Restaurant...it was located across from the tavern on Mulberry & Green...next to the parking lot, and

Ding Ho Rest. was on the corner of Mulberry & Green...I don't remember Wah Hing Grocery.

37-The Youth of Newark Chinatown circa early 1930s, courtesy Ron Eng Young

38-World War 2, US Bond Parade on Broad Street, circa 1940's, courtesy Frank Eng.

Mrs. Mary Goon Fong of Newark shows citizenship paper which means, she said, "I can vote in American elections now."

39-Mary Fong started special classes for Newark Chinatown women to get their citizenship papers, late 1940's-50's, courtesy Newark Public Library.

40-The Mon Family in front of the Newark Post Office Flag Pole 1940's. The Post Office was a well known family picture taking spot. Courtesy Frank Eng.

41-Frank Eng as a young boy with sister Joyce in glasses and friend Anna Chin, courtesy Frank Eng.

42-Pan Moo, Frank Eng's great aunt in front of what became the City's Carpenter shop but at that time housed Chinese, circa 1930's, courtesy Frank Eng.

43- *Mr and Mrs Kee Chee with 2 yr old Ben Kee Chee, big brother Jim, and the "Kee Chee Girls" as they were called, in front of The Newark Post Office, Courtesy Bob Lee*

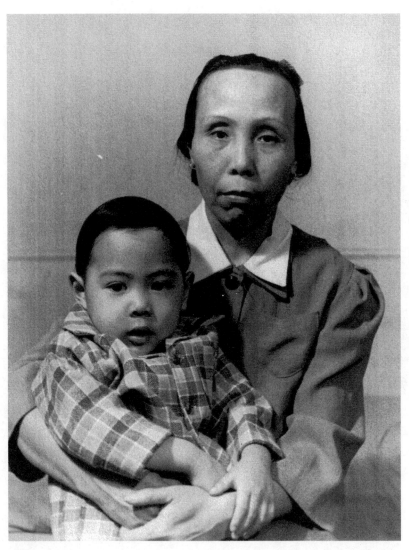

44-Mother of Wally and Frank Soo Hoo with son, circa 1940's, courtesy Frank Soo Hoo.

45-Norma Eng Wong and family, circa 1950's, courtesy Bob Lee.

46--Priscilla Eng Wong, left, sister Patricia, daughters of Norma Eng Wong and See Gat Eng Wong owners of the Shanghai Restaurant, pose at doorway of Sun Wo Yuen Co., grocery/herbal suppliers, and basement level Canton Restaurant, on Mulberry St. near Green, August 30, 1964, courtesy Newark Public Library

52-Frank on left and brother Wally Soo Hoo during interview, circa 2004, courtesy of the author.

PART 8

THE LAST GENERATION

47-The Mysterious Joe Fong on right, circa 1940's, courtesy NJ Historical Society

48- The Mysterious Joe Fong and wife sitting on stoop of possibly 69 Green Street. circa 1940's courtesy NJ Historical Society

I

THE MYSTERIOUS JOE FONG

The biggest mystery in Newark Chinatown was Joe Fong. Every time I tried to find Joe Fong someone had avoided the question or given me a short answer, or denied knowing a person named Joe Fong, and no one recognized his photo. Funny though, I first met Joe Fong in the New Jersey Historical Society. I had gone there to do my research on the project and had told the girl I was interested in any photos of Chinese they could find in their archives. She brought me one picture of a restaurant on Broad Street and then she came back with a group of photos which she claimed was filed under the title "An African-American Family." I guessed the reason why it was filed that way was because most of the pictures in the grouping included African-American women or men together with what seemed to be Caucasian or mixed-race persons.

I thumbed through the photos and as soon as I touched them I knew I had come across something very extraordinary. One photo was of Joe Young and another young man who may have been his brother, and it was from their dress obviously the late thirties or early forties. There was also a picture of Joe standing in front of a laundry that said Fong's laundry. Standing with him with her arm through his was a young "mulatto" (as she was described by a Chinatown male I interviewed) woman. She was beautiful, and if Joe had fallen for her, and I think he did, I could easily see why. Where she came from I do not know to this day. She remains a mystery. Someone had given the photos to the New Jersey Historical Society and the society had not made any record of who donated the photos, and what date they were given, or where they came from. Nothing was recorded. The photos were then locked up under the title an African American family until I came and asked to see all the photos they had on record. Strange enough however, that the young intern had stumbled on these photos at the same time I was doing my research and showed them to me on the day I came to the society. She said she had found them among the items she was currently cataloguing, but did not know any information about them. I was shocked when I first saw the photos. It was like looking at my own life. The man in the picture could have been my grandfather and the woman my grandmother or another member of my family or even my mother. The young child that appeared in these photos could have been I. She was obviously the offspring of the Chinese man and this mulatto woman. It was also obvious that I had photos of Joe as he passed through several phases of his life on Mulberry Street as the husband or mate of this mulatto woman and the father of this half Chinese young girl. I had to find out more about this couple, about Joe Fong and this store he stood in front of which carried the number 69. I went to every street in the neighborhood and every building looking for a 69 and couldn't find a 69. Where could this have been?

I asked Frank Eng. He stated that he remembered a Joe Fong who had married an African-American girl and had had a child, but he did not know where or when they moved out of Chinatown, he also could not tell me how to find the Fongs. One day I was interviewing Bea Soo Hoo and he looked at the photo and owned up to seeing a resemblance to a young man who was married to a "beautiful mulatto" woman in the neighborhood and they had had a child. When I asked him where was number 69, he stared at the photo for a long time and thought for a while. It was obvious that in his head he was remembering every number on every house in the neighborhood, walking the streets again and looking at every number. He knew the neighborhood well. Finally he looked at me, and then he said, "It must have been Green Street." That was the biggest opener for me to date in the Joe Fong saga. But where is Joe Fong and where is that girl who now would be the same age as myself and look like the spitting image of me. Where is she?

Although nobody knew Joe Fong, there were some who remembered Victor Fong, the son of Mrs. Mary Fong, whose picture appeared in the Newark Evening News during the 40's, sitting on a Chinese chest with a Thanksgiving cornucopia around her and who encouraged all the Newark Chinese women to get their citizenship papers.

49-Mary Fong and Family, circa 1950's, courtesy Frank Eng.

II

INTERVIEW WITH VICTOR FONG

AND WIFE GLORIA FONG

Victor Fong's mother's Chinese name was Ging Gee Fong. She was born in China and came over at age 12. His father came over via Peru in the late 1920s and went back to China a few times. Victor's family is from Toisan, mother from Song She-ung in what is known today as Guong Zhu.

Yoland: Did you ever go to China with your family?

Victor: Yes I went back once when I was very young but in early 1930s. But we fled back to the U.S. because we knew the Sino Japanese war was about to break out. I went with mother and father.

My father came back early. We intended to stay to early thirties but left because of the war. We came back on a ship called President Taft. I was two or three years old. But I was born in Newark.

My family felt that everyone was no good, the Italians were no good, the blacks were no good, the whites were no good, the only ones who were good were ones from the same village in China...I went to Lafayette Street School, and Newark College of Engineering, majored in chemical engineering, I was rather isolated from Chinatown playmates.

My favorite playmate was black kid who lived next door named William Edwards. I thought we were very good friends because we were friendly enough to throw ethnic slurs at each other in fun. I graduated from high school in 1947. I was pretty much out of touch with the Chinatown community. I hung out with kids from the west side of town. It was a very ordinary Chinatown; it still had its restaurants. Mrs. Black was there, her grocery was there, Brody's was there. Pinto had a restaurant just below #191. He and my father didn't get along. Ding Ho, the small restaurant on Green Street came in the early 1950s, sometime between 1951 and 1957. My mother died of diabetes and she was living on Broad Street, northern part. There was an apartment complex there. My father passed on when they lived near Broad and Hill.

In the context of being a community activist, my mother helped a lot of people get their citizenship, if that was their objective; she also worked for United States Life Insurance. She got involved with Peddie Memorial Church and introduced the Chinese community to the church. I went to Peddie Memorial with her, the minister was very pro-active, he was proactive in the Chinese community. My mother was ahead of her time, she was definitely not a traditionalist and was quite avant garde in the Americanization of the people in Chinatown, especially the women, i.e. citizenship, (Mary Fong organized citizenship classes at Peddie Memorial Church for the women of Newark Chinatown). She started many church activities for the Chinese community at Peddie. There was also the Old First Presbyterian Church, and some in Chinatown went to First Presbyterian and some went to Peddie Memorial.

Yoland   Was there segregation?

Victor   I don't know...yes, there were separate services at First Presbyterian, but it may have been due to language.

Most of Mom's friends were outside Chinatown. Alma Sayer was one, church goers, she was so busy with the restaurant business that I don't recall any friends. The Fongs are a clan by themselves....Mons and Lees are paper name Engs....Fong name came from China. My father had no problem coming back and forth from China, he came via Peru. His father did not own a restaurant as far as I know. Anyone who spoke English without an accent was considered legal. My grandfather went back and forth and my grandmother came over too. My grandfather was blind....my grandmother was Ah Paw. By the time she came over I was in my twenties, living at 191 Mulberry, then in late 1930s I moved to 222 Mulberry Street, next to Young's laundry.

I remember the Kuomintang Hall on Mulberry Street; (the building now houses the N.J. Law Journal and has the date 1923 on top) it had steps that resembled the New York brown stones. My father was an ac-

tivist in the Kuomintang; he was also the editor of the Chinese nation-
alists daily that came out of New York. My father's father and uncle
came from South America to Boston as a student. As I remember Chinatown went from Lafayette Street down Mulberry Street and not quite
to Elm Street and people lived on the side streets east of Mulberry like
Green, Elm, Columbia…but if you ask for boundaries you get a lot of
different answers….not very many people lived west of Mulberry.
Lafayette was filled with drunks, and mostly commercial.

    The railroad was there during my life time…where does Jersey
Central have its lines now?

Yoland: There is no Jersey Central now.

Victor: There is no Jersey Central now. That Jersey Central played an important
role in the Chinese community recreational lifestyle. A lot of people
hopped that train to Bradley Beach and Asbury Park and Belmar and the
shore points and there were places they were not allowed to go. New
Jersey beaches and things were segregated to all but whites at that time.

Yoland   Were there any restaurants in Chinatown that were segregated?

Victor   The Far Eastern next door had a white side and a black side and that's
the only one that I know of; there were two entrances.

Yoland   Gloria, how did you come to Chinatown?

Gloria: We had some boarders in our house that were Chinese and that is how
I came there, one of them said there was a job at the rice bowl.

Victor: Restaurants changed hands and ownership in Chinatowns like revolving
doors and they keep the same name. My mom and dad had managed
that place (though they owned the building) on more than on one occasion, and they had owners in between.

Yoland: When Gloria came to work at the restaurant, were you still working
there?

Gloria: I guess—no, he was living upstairs with his family.

Yoland: How did you two meet?

Gloria: He came down to the restaurant.

Victor: I checked her out, liked it.

Yoland: What did you do?

Victor: We teamed up.

Yoland: Did your family feel that it was okay for the two of you to get together?

Victor: No.

Yoland: Even your avant-garde mother?

Victor: Let me tell you something more about my mother. The proverbial thumb hit the fan. My mother was a kind of dichotomy because the culture and Christianity did not mix…so it was a dichotomy. The Chinese culture and Christian beliefs just don't mix well. Somehow she lived with that situation all her life. The Chinese culture is very male-oriented where Christianity is a more democratic life style or religion.

Yoland: And how did that fit in with Gloria?

Victor: You have to ask her that yourself.

Yoland: Are you saying that from a Christian point of view it was okay to date Gloria, but from a Chinese point of view it was not?

Victor: In that oversimplified context, yes.

Yoland: What did she say to you?

Victor: I'd rather not remember (he laughs).

Yoland: What about your father, what did he say?

Victor: On my mother's side, we were outcasts.

Gloria: Victor and his family were estranged from about 1947 to about 1951.

Once we got together the family didn't have anything to do with us until after my son was born, and then they invited us to come live in Chinatown and that's when we started living in Chinatown. We had been living with my family on 10th Street. My family didn't care.

Yoland: Was your father glad that you were marrying a Chinese man?

Gloria: Not particularly, because there were westerners that made more money.

Yoland: Victor, when I interviewed other Chinatown people who remembered you, they painted you as a very wild young man who had run away from home and came back very worldly.

Victor: Having gone off, having come back is true, whether you could equate that to the acquisition of worldliness is something else. I left Chinatown at seventeen; Gloria and I ran away together. We knew we weren't going to be accepted so it seemed to us we didn't have much of a choice, so we went to South Carolina.

Yoland: Why South Carolina?

Victor: It was a state that had liberal age requirements for marriage, waiting period, blood test, all that kind of crap. Five years later we went back to the place where we got married and it wasn't the same.

Yoland: So here you are in South Carolina, and you have to find a place to live and a job. What did you do?

Victor: When you're young you have this feeling of invincibility and immortality and we didn't need to get a job down there. We needed to get a job in New Jersey since that was where we wanted to be.

Gloria: We returned to New Jersey a day or so later and we went by way of Virginia where I had relatives, then we came back home. We went to my mother's house; my mother knew what was going on.

Victor: We were welcome there much more than my mom and dad's.

Gloria: And that's the story of our lives together.

Yoland: That is very exciting.

Victor: We were rebels.

Gloria: I didn't have much of a family. My father was Chinese and I stayed with him most of the time. My mother and he were always not together, not till I was thirty. My father was born in China, came to U.S. in 1906, the year of the fire, and he said he was six and I think they were wetbacks. They came illegally; he came with his uncle to San Francisco and I don't know when he came to the East Coast.

Yoland: Wasn't it unusual for your father to get together with a woman who was not Chinese? Did you feel any discomfort about your racial background?

Gloria: Lots. There wasn't anyone else around that was half American Indian and half Chinese, so you weren't accepted anywhere.

Yoland: What kind of challenges did you face?

Gloria: I was a loner, still a loner.

Victor: When I was going to college, I was going to college with working people. When I was going to high school, there were a few others but I don't remember their names. Is my East Side yearbook here?

Gloria: No!

Victor: Robert Soo Hoo is my generation; I had lots of fights with him. There was a Caucasian society in the high school and they were apathetic; they didn't care who I was married to, they were half Italian and half Polish. In Newark, most of the Italians are Sicilian, but most of the Italians in New England are non-Sicilians and there is regional prejudice in Italy from way back, where a Sicilian wasn't even considered an Italian and they would call them an Ethiopian, meaning they were black...and the Newark Italians were Sicilian and they are an entirely different people from the Italians, like the ones you find in New England.

Yoland: Gloria, what nationality of friends did you have when you were growing up?

Gloria: Black, white, and I would hang out with each group at different times. I went to Rhode Island Junior College here. I had my first child when I was sixteen. His parents did not care for the fact that I was pregnant before we got married. All my children were born in Newark. My first child was a girl. The youngest was a year when we moved out of Newark to Somerville for seven years and in 1964 we moved to New England. When the kids were little we lived on Mulberry Street at #222.

Victor: I worked in Somerville for RCA. It wasn't hard for me to get a job, I was raised so that we never played the race card and I was never affected in jobs by race. I worked for Bell Labs, now known as Lucent Tech. Because I was a semi-conductor tech, which was a skill that most people didn't have, I was able to find work. I really don't think it was hard for Chinese men to get jobs in the New Jersey community. Chinese culture is very pro-education, so you went to college or you were nothing, so your family pushed you, oh yeah!

Yoland: How old were you when you started at NJIT?

Victor: I was class of 1960; it took me nine years to get through so I guess 1951

Yoland: So you and Gloria were already together?

Victor: Yeah. I went to night school, worked at Bell Labs, and then RCA; tuition wasn't very expensive at that time. My family helped to the extent that we lived in the same building as the restaurant, which was a big help.
            My mother was the first Chinese woman in New Jersey to get her citizenship because they passed the law while we were living there; before that they didn't allow Chinese to get citizenship.

III

SO MUCH TO QUESTION

AND SO LITTLE TIME TO TELL IT

There are a lot more characters I could write about in my story of all the people who lived, passed through or were connected to Newark Chinatown. There is Harry Li Sooey, the younger, who gave me his family tree and spent hours talking and rambling, but not answering my questions. Harry would tell me no stories about his youth or his family. Later on I wondered if it was because his father chased all the women in Newark Chinatown and ran one of the biggest gambling establishments on Mulberry Street. After people left Newark Chinatown they did not want their families or their success to be connected to things that would be seen as having negative connotations in the middle class American societies with which they wanted to be connected.

Then there was Mr. Mon, who was considered to be one of the most respected elders, an incredible inventor, photographer, business man. His family was responsible for getting many of the Newark Chinese out of China during the change over from Manchu to Mao. Jackie, his youngest son, was the only string I had to him, but Jackie also refused to give me any facts. He did give me many of the family items I now have in the Newark Chinatown Collection, which we have exhibited and some of which we have given to NYU archives.

There was Joe Young, the fabulous Joe Young who danced like he was sixteen when he was in his nineties. Who came to work in Newark Chinatown at the age of thirteen. His son and daughter worked with him on his autobiography, which we published in one of the Newark Chinatown reunion booklets, and which, with their permission, I have included here.

50-Joe Young age 12, 1922 just before leaving China, courtesy Ron Eng Young.

51-Joe Eng Young, age 12, 1922 just before leaving China, courtesy Ron Eng Young.

IV

JOSEPH ENG YOUNG,

AS TOLD TO SON RONALD ENG YOUNG

(copyright Ron Young 2005)

I, Joe Young (Joseph Eng Young) now 94 years old, came from China in 1922 at the age of 12. I settled in Newark Chinatown and lived in a laundry on Pennington Street. I went to grade school near Chinatown. On Sundays I would attend Sunday School, sometimes going to two different churches, in order to learn English along with the Bible. I often saw Allan Eng-Achson, then known as Allan Lum Chee. I was baptized Joseph Eng at Peddie Memorial Baptist Church on Broad Street.

When I was 15, I worked at Eagle Restaurant, located on the second floor of 158 Market Street, where I was first an apprentice in the kitchen. Then when I reached the legal age, I began working as a bus boy and a waiter. I attended Newark Technical School in the evening while working at Eagle Restaurant during lunch hour. I was living in the laundry and did whatever chores necessary to help. At night and every spare moment I studied English with the help of a Chinese dictionary. In the daytime when business was slow, the waiters, many of whom were college students from China helped me learn English. This went on for a few years while I was growing up.

I then went to New York to Stewart Automobile School for practical training in automobile mechanics, receiving a certificate in 1927. I also went to Chamberlain School, a small private school in Brooklyn just to study English.

While working at Globe Restaurant on Broad Street during lunchtime, I studied at Newark Technical School in the evening, studying Math, English, and technical subjects for about six years.

By 1931, I was accepted at Tri-State College in Angola, Indiana, to study Engineering. Tri-State had four quarter sessions and accepted students with unusual backgrounds from all over the world. I went with Joseph Mon of Newark Chinatown. We also bought and fixed up a car that Joe Mon used for a trip back to Newark to visit his wife and young child. In 1934 I graduated with B. S. in Mechanical Engineering.

I then took a one-year course in airplane and engine mechanics at Casey Jones School of Aeronautics, Newark, on Broad Street, opposite Washington Park, and worked as a waiter at Globe Restaurant, nearby, on weekends. All the years I went to night school, I had worked at Globe Restaurant lunchtime. In 1936 I was hired by Couse Laboratories in East Orange to develop their mobile machine shop. War developed and the U.S. Government contracted Couse to manufacture a mobile maintenance machine shop for use in the Burma Road. Couse moved to 300 Passaic Street, Newark, for that production. I worked there for nine years until the end of the war when Couse Laboratories closed.

I then worked at various places, such as Weldotron, U.S. Tool Co., Bendix Aviation, China Motors, Conmar, as a draftsman, designer, and engineer, retiring in 1975 at age 65 from Westinghouse Electric in Bloomfield as an engineer.

On June 1, 1940, I married Alice Bo-Goon Moy of N. Y. Chinatown, a graduate of N.Y.U. One of our ushers was Wallace Seto Wey of Newark Chinatown. We lived on Oliver Street near Chinatown for almost two years, then moved with our 6 months old son, Ronald, to live at Bradley Court in Vailsburg, a new housing project for defense workers. I was a volunteer air raid warden evenings and weekends. We lived at Bradley Court for 14 years. We then bought our house on Pine Grove Terrace in Vailsburg. We lived there until 1981 when we moved to Long Island to live with our daughter, Linda Joe, and her family.

We were all active at Kilburn Memorial Presbyterian Church on South Orange Avenue. Ron and Judy graduated from West Side High School, Linda and Allan from Vailsburg High. They were all honor students. We were proud to attend their graduation from college, Ron, Ph.D. - M.I.T., Judy, College of Wooster, Ohio, Linda, University of Pennsylvania, Philadelphia, and Allan, Brooklyn Polytechnic Institute, Brooklyn.

We were also proud to attend the graduation of our four grandchildren, Ron and Jean's son, Evan, and their daughter, Lauren, from Harvard University, Linda's two daughters, Miranda from Hood College, Maryland, and Bernadette from Binghamton University, Binghamton, N. Y. Evan received his MBA from Stanford University in California June 2000 and Lauren also received her MBA from Stanford June 2003.

Allan and Lucy's son, Jeffrey, graduated from Simons Rock College of Bard College, Massachusetts, at the age of 18 with an Associate's Degree, and is now studying Music at Oberlin. Their 16-year-old son, Nicholas, attends LaGuardia High School of Performing Arts in Manhattan. It has been 82 years since I arrived in Newark Chinatown and 65 years June 1st when Alice and I celebrate our wedding anniversary. I appreciate all the help and opportunities I have received along the way making it possible for me to have a wonderful life with my family.

Joseph Eng Young passed away on August 9, 2008, opening night of China Olympics.

V

More and More and More

Joe Young's' story represents not just his story but the story of all of Newark Chinatown's families. There are the Kee Chees. When I first went to interview Ben Kee Chee, he told me he did not know anything about the history of Newark Chinatown and he would not talk about his family. Much later on as he got to know me we became good friends, but I never got the real story from him and I regret that I could never get a moment with his sisters who everyone felt were the highlight of Newark Chinatown. He did help very much with his memories of how Newark Chinatown looked and his visual recordings helped us a lot with the models we made of Newark Chinatown.

I had so many more questions for Wally Soo Hoo, who as a young teenager was surviving on the streets of 1900's Newark Chinatown but he passed away before I could have asked them all. We never realize what we have when we have it and no matter what we do after it's gone, we always feel we could have done so much more.

The height of Newark Chinatown and all the Chinatowns that ever existed was when the young Chinese men cut their queues, put on their western clothes, saw themselves in the mirror and shaped their dreams into the magazine and film images of the silent era and then the talking films like "Little Caesar" (1930), "Public Enemy" (1931). If they couldn't go to the movies because they weren't allowed to, I am sure they may have listened to the radio advertisements, the radio drama detective stories like "Boston Blackie", and examined the magazines that created the aura for which they thirsted, the feeling of being in control, the feeling of power in their powerless world. Did these All-American characters merge into their psyches and get played out in the gangster style killings of the Tongs. Chinese women also had their own reveries, buying hats with seductive short pull down front veils, hair styled short, or with permed curls or waves. Anna May Wong must surely have won the hearts of her Chinese sisters as they saw her movie images in which she fell in love with white men she could not have. American life changed Chinese women allowing their matriarchal power to surface, even though they could only do it within their own families. Norma Eng Wong was one of these women. There was a sense of false freedom for all and since young Chinese men could easily join the tongs and live out their fantasies, many of them did. Others worked in restaurants when they weren't fantasizing, washing, cooking or serving till late hours into the night. Then the wars came, first one, then two, and it was all over, the reality changed, the struggle changed, citizenship brought some wonderful gifts, but it also brought the end of Newark Chinatown.

LOOKING FOR CHINATOWN ⁃ 9

Eat a Cup of Tea by Louis Chu

When I first read Louis Chu's book, it was several years after seeing the movie and at that time I was not aware that there had been a Chinatown in Newark. When I read it a second time it was because I was not only searching for clues to Newark Chinatown but I was looking for, specific characters and details that could help me piece my story together. By the third time I read the book, I had found what I was looking for but I was also aware of how Chu had merged both the Newark Chinatown and the New York Chinatown into one city, one family. The characters in Chu's book could be the characters of either city but the places he talks about rang some bells with the stories I had heard about Newark. On Green Street in Newark, walking toward McCarter Highway, just before you arrive at Columbia, was the last basement club house in Newark Chinatown. Actually it was the last gambling club house before Chinatown fell. This was where gamblers and non-gamblers hung out. The old men of Newark Chinatown used to meet here to talk and watch the game being played. This was the meeting place of the last generation of Newark Chinatown bachelor society and I think Chu used this basement club house as the one in his book. Chu would have had to have known about this club house and may have frequented it himself, to hang out to watch these old guys speaking in their Toisanese dialect, hear them tell stories about their past or just haggle with each other in friendly camaraderie. Still standing, the house has seen many owners since that time. It is now covered in pale green aluminum siding and is still fairly well kept. The basement where the club house existed recently housed a couple whose demeanor suggested drug addiction. They had a beautiful calico cat. The woman would sit outdoors on many occasions and stroke it in her arms.

One Sunday as my husband and I walked my dog Ming, the cat emerged from the basement stair, saw the dog, and dog saw cat. I had let the dog off his leash so he could go into the empty lot across from the house. As the cat emerged I was reconnecting the leash. At the moment their eyes met, Ming sprung out of my hand and he took off across the street towards the cat. The cat turned into the alley between the houses and the dog took off after him. Both my husband and I, followed by the cat owner chased after the pair. By the time I got hold of my dog, the cat was cornered in the basement window sill and my dogs head seemed to be grabbing at him. I pulled his collar to yank him back and noticed a large clump of fur in his mouth. Since my dog is the same color as the cat, unless you knew where mouth ended and fur began, you couldn't tell that his mouth was filled with golden cat fur. I pulled his face away from the direction of the cat owner, and dragged him behind me, hearing the scream-ing woman's words following me down the alley. Luckily she had not seen the mouthful of fur. "You almost killed my cat," she screamed, as she picked up her animal and began to soothe the terrified beast. I dragged Ming down the street reprimanding him for his behavior and apologizing loudly and profusely; try-ing to get the dog as far away from the scene of the crime as possible. My husband stayed behind to talk and calm the excited woman and her husband who had come running out from the basement.

It has been several years now since that incident; meanwhile the neighborhood has gone through another change. The empty lot now has a huge two family house on it, in which the new wave of Mexican immigrants live. The basement apartment seems empty since I never see anyone going in and out anymore. The neighborhood must have always been a neighborhood of change because it seems to be a springboard for illegals, new immigrants and shady characters.

This city had sprung up around the old farms and the farm-ers had started moving to the suburbs. City life had brought with it all the things that it had in Europe: women of the streets, the poor and beggars, the lower classes, new arrivals from other countries or other cities who needed to find work. This area behind city hall hadn't changed much since it had become the area behind where the city conducted its business. This was where people came because it was close to all the official offices, rooms were cheap, and it was the perfect place for restaurants and laundries. Perhaps it is also the best place to hide if you are an illegal, right under the nose of the law.

In my interview with eighty-nine-year-old Wallace Soo Hoo or Wallace Seto Wey as Joe Young called him, and his brother Frank, we spoke about Chinatown's Green Street club and other Chinatown's social clubs. Frank said, "You have to remember back in those days because Asian peoples couldn't mix with the other people, they got together and formed social clubs and every year the clubs had a volley ball team that would go to New York City Chinatown to compete against other teams. Newark Chinatown had a club and we had parades down Broad Street with the Dragon and Lion Dances too." I found this quite remarkable.

How Ming Chow Died
February 22, 2005
My Dear Aunt Ah Choy and Aunt Ah Moy,
Wednesday February 19, 2005, was a beautiful day. The temperature was in the 60s, and the buds on the trees were being fooled by Mother Nature into thinking spring had begun. The warm sun and clear skies made me save my dog walking for the height of the day's temperature. So, around 2:30 p.m., I buckled up my dog Ming Chow with his harness, put on my coat, no hat, and went for a long walk. Ming was ecstatic and as usual headed for the park. He sniffed at everything. At each tree he stopped to indulge himself in momentary fantasies about the dogs whose odor permeated his nostrils. Everything and everyone was moving very slowly, or so it seemed, like a day described in a song. We made our way down Elm Street, past the ghost of the Chinese laundries of the past, down McWhorter and up Walnut to the park. It was filled with children just out of school, playing hockey and soccer on the same court. I looked up at the sun through the trees in the park and allowed it to caress my winterized face, melting the cares and wrinkles into a soft, serene calm.

247

Slowly Ming Chow and I made our way down the path. He, sniffing and following trails of scent, me, raising my face to accept the sun at every stop he made. The path rounded its way past the hokey players who were relinquishing the court to the soccer youth, now increased in numbers. We slowly followed it past the children's play area, where mothers helped little ones up slide ladders and older children stopped to watch Ming Chow as he sniffed, moving in their direction. He paid them absolutely no attention, deeply involved in the scent of the moment. We rounded the corner near the bathrooms and the water fountain, still turned off for the winter, and came to the basketball court where every high school boy and girl was throwing balls into hoops independent of each other. The baseball field was empty as usual except for a derelict fellow who stood guarding it and having a conversation with an invisible friend, while listening to a radio or some kind of noise from the wire attached to his ear. He was a frightening looking fellow so I pulled Ming from going in any direction that would take us too close to him. We rounded the last curve in the walk at the bottom of the park and headed towards the basketball court where all the immigrant Hispanic males played volleyball. They were out in full force, playing a game that they strictly policed, their coats off, their shirts clinging to their bodies with sweat, their wild hair flying back and forth in their face as they jumped and pushed the ball across the net, first one way then the other. So they continued for hours on end. Weekends were the big days and you could bet on one team or another. Early Saturday and Sunday mornings the tournaments lasted all day. When a man tired he was replaced with another. Today they were basking their brown bodies in the warm spring like sun as they moved to and fro batting, pushing the ball. They were practicing for the summer days to come. Ming did not seem to be tiring and he was determined to inspect every area of the park, but I pulled him onto the track that led up and out of the park, just in case he had some trouble making it back home. He was sixteen years old now and sometimes the walk to, around the park and back home was a very tiring one for him. We exited the park and slowly headed down New York Avenue. It was about six blocks to McWhorter Street, and although he had used up all the urine in his body, he kept trying to leave remnants of his smell at every tree. It had been a long time since we had come this way so he was forced to renew his mark to let every animal know that this was still his terrain. At McWhorter we made a right turn to head back to Lafayette and home. I was in a dazed mood from the sun, the warmth of such a beautiful day and the enjoyment of the walk with Ming, watching him again and again stop to hound out another smell, like he was on the trail of a wild animal. We reached the corner of Elm and McWhorter and I continued on, crossing the street in my daze, not realizing that Ming was not with me. The leash stretched back behind, but in my daze I was completely unaware of it. Something made me turn and when I did I saw a car race by me and Ming rolling out from under it. I screamed and ran to him. He was bleeding from the mouth and nose. I began to scream and scream and by now all the people who had seen the crime came towards me. One man ran after the car trying to get the taxi's license plate with his camera cell phone. I told another to use his cell phone to call my husband and tell him to come with the car and take us to the hospital. Ming Chow continued to bleed and howl in pain still trying to get up. I was in agony as I watched the blood flowing from him onto the street forming a pool of red clotting mass. I held him and tried to keep him from moving as we waited for the car to arrive. Someone wanted to call 911 and an ambulance, but I reminded him that this was a dog and an ambulance would not come for a dog. Everyone was in as much anguish as I was seeing the animal in such pain and discomfort. Anger at the driver who had sped away was in the voices of the people around me. My husband Hal arrived and we got the dog into the rear of the station wagon. Over the back seat I held him down and tried to talk to him, but he tried to get up and press his head to the walls of the car, crying out and bleeding profusely. I began to die inside of me then. I had let my dog down. I was not paying attention when we crossed the street. I had gone into one of my dazes. I had beamed away from reality and caused an accident. I had caused my dogs pain. We got to the vet and he gave him some injections of morphine to settle him and stop the bleeding. He gave us a stretcher and told us how to get to the animal hospital. We got back into the car and drove like the devil, following the written instructions given us by the vet. At the animal hospital they admitted us right away and took Ming into the area for treatment. Hal and I sat outside waiting. I was weeping at my foolishness, my lack of awareness, my selfishness; my stupidity was now causing my dog so much pain. I called my night teaching job and tried to get out of going to work, but they wouldn't hear about it. It was just a dog. No one cared about the lives of dogs. They were not humans, so their lives had much less value. How could an animal be in the affections of a human in such a way to cause unsoothable grief. I anguished as we sat and waited. Finally they came out and told us there was not much else they could do but wait. He would be in critical condition for 48 hours. We would have to wait. Hal and I left. I was inconsolable. The guilt I carried and still carry has been like a hammer pounding at my brain. We returned that evening to the hospital after I had left work but he was not better. We petted him and soothed him because although he was sedated, we knew he would know we were there. We left and the next morning I called. He had made it through the night but was still on the very critical list. Hal felt for sure that since he was fighting so valiantly he would make it and I allowed myself to believe this. That afternoon we went back to the hospital after I returned from my morning teaching position. He was more awake than before but he was in so much more pain. We spent some time talking to him and softly soothing him, whispering encouraging words. He tried to get up to be with us and I had to tell him to stay. He became calmer once he heard my voice say this, then he rose up and spoke to me about his discomfort. He did it in the way he often talked to me in a gargled breath of sounds and tones and then he lay down again. I told him what a good dog he was. I told him that he was the best dog in the world. I told him how much I loved him and I told him that he should stay and get better and that we would be waiting to take him home. After he calmed down we left the hospital. I knew I would not be able to get back there again until tomorrow since I had a full night of teaching. By the time we got home, there was a call from the hospital. He had passed away right after we left. I went into a state of shock. But I wanted to see him once more. I called in to my job and stated firmly that I would not be in that night. We drove back to the hospital from which we had just come and spent an hour watching him and soothing his lifeless form that already was becoming stiff. His fur was still warm and I clipped a piece to keep with me forever. I had to let Hal take care of all the details about his cremation. How could I have let my good friend down this way? This dog had been sent by the ancestors to protect me, appearing on my door step, eleven years ago, and now he was gone, out of my life, in one instant. I knew I would grieve for a long time.

Your niece, Yoland

It was my dog Ming Chow, who was sent to lead me to the Newark Chinatown, and now my dog was gone. It was time to end this constant searching…..it was time for someone else to pick up the rest of the history. (the building now houses the N.J. Law Journal and has the date 1923 on top)

CONCLUSION

I

THE FINAL DESTRUCTION

OF NEWARK CHINATOWN

It was the summer of 2000 when I opened the Wrought Iron Gate, entered through it, and locked it behind me. Walking through the narrow alley way, I felt the rush of cool air, ducked to avoid the circling flies and hurried to get to the end of the red brick walls on either side of me. They echoed of times past and as I entered into the small turn of the century garden I felt a rush of peace and I knew I was home. On my right, my thick patch of celery shone green and beckoned to be harvested. My bodhisattva sitting under the apple tree, with her leg propped up, and her lips spouting soft liquid water into the fountain on whose edge she perched, seemed to be humming a one syllable tone, which was really the sound of the water falling into itself. I sat down in the grass green lounge chair and looked up at the house I had given back its life.

Abandoned in 1998, the building stood on what was once the Baldwin farm. The Baldwin family had built townhouses on the farm property for members of the younger generations of Baldwins, around the turn of the century, when it was obvious that the farm era had ended. My husband and I had purchased the building from a Chinese family in 1998 and started stripping it to its original self, replacing the outer walls which were buckled and about to fall off and repairing the leaky roof. I felt I had made a connection to the past that hung ghostly in the neighborhood, but which I knew nothing about. The house and its spirits called to me constantly, telling me what to fix and how to repair them. I had stripped the wooden floors spending hours, removing tar used to glue down the early tiles, and had come upon the brown stained boards from the original days. Only then could I get the sander to work across the old and beautiful wood. I started stripping the decorative carved wooden front doors, with the glass panes over which hung the old lace curtains. I could not bring myself to take them down, and instead had washed and starched them to bring back the life. One morning I received a letter in the mail that the neighborhood had been "blighted" and slated for redevelopment. It was a complete shock. I had never heard of a neighborhood becoming "blighted" and so could not understand. I had no knowledge of the laws of eminent domain. The city was moving to take my beautiful home. Time stopped for me then. My husband and I stopped working on the restoration and prepared ourselves for a political fight.

As I sat in the green chair in the garden, the squirrel came down the tree and moved to the edge of the old well and began to bury his winter meal. On the other side of the wall surrounding the garden, I heard the automobiles pulling in and out in the newly built parking lot that had destroyed the natural habitat of millions of insects and small animals, not to mention the birds and bees which propagated the fruit trees in my yard and the yard of my neighbor, Elsa. Elsa was from Ecuador; she owned a food truck stand that parked in the down town area and provided lunch for the office workers. She and her husband had saved their pennies to buy their home and had made extensive renovations in it. She also was now faced with having to move.

My house stood on what once was the Baldwin farm. The Baldwins were one of the founding families who settled Newark in the 1600s. After several generations the farm was broken up into lots and family members inherited parcels. The old farmhouse was kept until 1906, when it was torn down to build a fire station which stood on the corner of Mulberry and Lafayette. This was the area in which the city of Newark was founded. This was the area in which the city now made plans to build a hockey arena with a massive television complex to televise the games.

My house was built as a one family town house, with bedrooms on the second floor, living and sitting rooms on the first and a maid's apartment on the third floor. The fireplaces on the first floor were ornate with simply carved black marble facings and a mantel piece. The fireplace on the second floor had been removed and the wall closed. The only hint of its existence was the broken tiles on the floor where it once stood. The rooms were fairly spacious and the closets very large. The house had been altered several times. During the 1920s it was a rooming house, as were all of the houses in the area. Later on it was turned into three apartments, one on each floor.

The entire neighborhood of brick and wooden frame Victorian houses sprung up during the 1800s, America's magic era. One house remained that dated back to the farm period and it had seen many changes in ownership. I loved walking the streets of the neighborhood and living in the fantasy of each era as I had researched it to have been. I had gone to the historical society and talked to everyone, taping their stories, and had created maps of all the possible changes I could find.

Now I had to fight a major battle to keep something I loved. My father had always said as we were growing up, that a man hadn't lived until he had owned and worked a piece of the earth for himself. Was this my piece of the earth that I would fight to the death to keep? Or would I take a Native American attitude that I didn't own anything anyway and let go? It remained to be seen, since I didn't know at the time that it would take five or more years of fighting and living in turmoil and anxiety. No one seemed to feel the significance of the surroundings I now existed in, no one seemed to care about the history I was unraveling. Yes, the historians responded, this was a historic area, but since they weren't doing the digging, why should they care. There was no fame and no money for them in fighting this battle; as a matter of fact they, like I, had more to lose, as a result of going against "the machine" that was this city and their proposed investments.

The systematic destruction of Chinatown began a long, long time before they tore down the arcade. Did it begin when they tore down the Fair Street buildings, and renamed Fair Street into Lafayette Street to make everyone forget? Or did it begin in the 1950s when they tried to condemn everything in the Mulberry Street and Lafayette Street area, and William Cone tried to photograph it before it was all gone. The desire to destroy Chinatown was an old idea that finally succeeded in the 1960's when all but the last Chinese families left. But in 2005, the last buildings were being destroyed in Mayor Sharpe James plan to build an arena for the Devils, New Jersey's hockey team. The fire station, built in 1906, was destroyed as this book was being completed; the arcade was destroyed in 1958.

In the 1940s, the owners of 206 and 210 Mulberry Street ordered Chinese tenants to move out of their apartments, after the police raided several of the apartments and arrested eighty-two men for gambling. Although most of the arrests were made in the Mulberry Arcade, the tenants of buildings on Mulberry Street were still given the eviction notices. The Newark Police threatened the Berry's Tavern Incorporation with closure of a building if gambling persisted on the premises. The owner claimed he had been advised by his attorney that this process was the best procedure and that he should cooperate with the police. The tenants, all whom were on month to month tenancy, were told that their tenancy was terminated June 30.

It is December 2006. The year 2007 is looming on the horizon and there is nothing but mud and steel and havoc in Newark Chinatown as the builders proceed with the hockey arena, despite the many newspaper articles stating there is no money to build this arena. As I plan my move out of the area, leaving Newark Chinatown, all I will have to look forward to are the yearly reunions we now have of all the Newark Chinatown residents and the continued effort to collect as much of the history that I can to preserve what is left for someone in the future who will become as excited as I did about Newark Chinatown.

Now it is 2010 and all the buildings that were the Mulberry Arcade and their foundations are no more. They have been bulldozed and blacktopped to make room for parking lots to service the Prudential Center New Jersey Devils Arena. The Arena has destroyed any remnant of the Chinatown that was a vibrant population of 3,000 at its height in the 1920s.

53-Chinatown Reunion 2003 held at NJ Historical Society in Newark, photograqpher Corky Lee.

54-Helen Zia, Newark born Chinese American author and activist speaking at Chinatown Reunion, 2003, photograqpher Corky Lee.

55-Richard Eng, President of Eng Association, New York City, speaking at 2003 Newark Chinatown Reunion held at NJ Historical Society, photograqpher Corky Lee.

56- *Leslie Eng (on right) questioning a participant at the Chinatown Reunion, photographer Corky Lee.*

57-*Chinatown Reunion 2003, NJ Historical Society, photographer Corky Lee.*

II

THE REUNIONS

There were five reunions all together. The first was held at the New Jersey Historical Society, under Sally Yerkovich. The other four were held wherever we could find a space that was not too expensive. At the reunions, people ate, danced an we had traditional Chinese entertainment. One year we had the Nai Ni Chen Dancers performing the Monkey King. The reunions were wonderful but every year we lost more and more and we could not interest the younger generations in continuing the history. The reunions were photographed by Corky Lee.

Some of his photographs are included here.

58- 2014 - The top of the Lun On Co building, a stone slab, now sits across from Prudential Arena on Mulberry Street, an invisible remnant of Newark Chinatown, courtesy of the author.

59- In 2014, Ben Young, Wally Soo Hoo and John Eng who grew up in Newark Chinatown, came back to see what was left after the building of the Prudential Arena, courtesy the author.

SELECTED BIBLIOGRAPHY

1. Asbury, Herbert. The Barbary Coast, An Informal History of San Francisco Underworld. New York, NY, Alfred A. Knopf: Thunder Mouth Press. 1933.
2. Booth, Martin. Dragon Syndicates, The Global Phenomenon of The Triads. New York, NY: Carol and Graff Publishers, 1999.
3. Carlson, Ellsworth. The Foochow Missionaries, 1847 – 1880. Cambridge, Mass: Harvard University Press. 1974
4. Chan, Sucheng. Asian Americans an Interpretive History, New York, NY: Simon and Schuster. 1991
5. Ching, Frank. Ancestors – 900 Years In The Life Of A Chinese Family. New York, NY: William Morrow and Co. 1988
6. Chu, Louis. Eat A Bowl Of Tea. New York, NY. 1961
7. Chu, Yiu. The Triads as Business. New York, NY: Routledge Press. 2000
8. Dawson, Raymond. The Chinese Chameleon, An Analysis of European Conceptions Of Chinese Civilization. London: Oxford University Press. 1967
9. Eberhard, Wolfram. Social Mobility in Traditional China. Leiden, Netherlands: EJ Brill. 1962
10. Farkas, Lani Ah Tye. Bury My Bones In America. Nevada City: Carl Mantz Publisher
11. Fay, Peter Ward. The Opium War 1840 – 1842. North Carolina: University of North Carolina Press. 1975
12. Feng, Ssu-yu and Ingalls, Jeremy. The Political History of China 1840 – 1928. Princeton, New Jersey: D. Van Nostrand Co. Inc. 1956
13. Fung, Yu-Lan. A Short History of Chinese Philosophy. New York, NY: The Tree Press of Simon and Schuster. 1948 and 1976
14. Hall, Bruce Edward. Tea That Burns. New York, NY: Free Press, Division of Simon and Schuster. 1998

15. Hoexter, Corinne. From Canton to California, The Epic of Chinese Immigration. New York, NY: 1976
16. Holbrook's Newark City and Business Directory: Holbrook's Steam Press, Newark NJ, years ending 1880 thru 1890.
17. Hurd, Douglas. The Arrow War, The Anglo-Chinese Confusion 1856 – 1860. New York, NY: Macmillan Co. 1967
18. Ierley, Merritt. A Place In History, North Arlington, New Jersey: North Arlington Free Public library. 1994
19. Kingston, Maxine Hong. Chinamen. New York, NY: Alfred A. Knopf. 1976
20. Kwong, Peter. Chinatown, New York. New York, NY: The New Press. 2001
21. Kwong, Peter. The New Chinatown. Canada Ltd: Harper Collins. 1987
22. Lee, Joanne Faung Jean. Asian Americans. New York, NY: The New Press. 1991
23. Lin, Jan. Deconstructing Chinatown, Ethnic Enclave, Global Change. New York, NY: The New Press. 1998
24. Meskill, John. The Pattern Of Chinese History. Boston: DC Heath and Co. 1966
25. Nee, Victor G. and Bret De Bary. Longtime California, A Documentary Study of An American Chinatown. New York, NY: Simon and Schuster. 1972
26. Preston, Diane. The Boxer Rebellion. New York, NY: Walker and Co. 2000
27. Reischauer, Edwin O. and Fairbank, John K. East Asia - The Great Tradition. Boston: Houghton Mifflin Co. 1958
28. Reischauer Edwin O and Fairbank, John K. History of East Asian Civilization. Boston: Houghton Mifflin. 1958
29. Ross, Rev. John. The Manchus. London: Elliot Stock. 1891
30. Salyer, Lucy. Laws Harsh As Tigers, Chinese Immigrants And The Shaping Of Modern Immigration Law. Chapel Hill, London: University of North Carolina Press. 1995
31. Siu, Paul C.P. Edited by Tchen, John Kuo Wei. The Chinese Laundryman, A Study of Social Isolation. New York and London: NYU Press. 1987
32. Takaki, Ronald. Strangers From A Different Shore, A History of Asian Americans. New York, NY: Little Brown and Co. 1989
33. Tchen, John Kuo Wei. New York Before Chinatown, Orientalism And The Shaping of American Culture 1776 – 1882. Baltimore and London: John Hopkins University Press. 1999
34. Teng, S.Y.. The Taiping Rebellion and The Western Powers, A Comprehensive Survey. London: Oxford at The Clarendon Press, 1971
35. Wakeman, Frederic. Strangers At The gate, Social Disorder In South China 1839 – 1861. Berkeley and Los Angeles: University Of California Press. 1966
36. Waley, Arthur. The Opium War Through Chinese Eyes. Great Britain: George

Allen and Unwin Ltd. 1958
37. Yin, Xiao-huang. Chinese American Literature Since The 1850's. Urbana and Chicago: University of Illinois Press. 2000
38. Yu, Renqin. To Save China, To Save Ourselves, The Chinese Hand Laundry Alliance of New York. Philadelphia, Temple University Press. 1992